It's in the Cards!

GETTING THE BIGGEST IMPACT FROM YOUR SMALLEST AD

It's in the Cards!

GETTING THE BIGGEST IMPACT FROM YOUR SMALLEST AD

Ivan R. Misner, Ph.D.
Candace Bailly
Dan Georgevich

PARADIGM PUBLISHING

It's in the Cards!

GETTING THE BIGGEST IMPACT FROM YOUR SMALLEST AD

A Paradigm Publishing Book.

To order the book, contact your local bookstore or call 800-688-9394.

ISBN 0-9740819-0-6 hardcover

The authors may be contacted at the following addresses:

Paradigm Publishing
BNI
199 S. Monte Vista, Suite 6
San Dimas, CA 91773-3080
800-825-8286 (outside So. Calif.)
909-305-1818 (in So. Calif.)
909-305-1811 fax

Ivan R. Misner, Ph.D.
misner@bni.com

Candace Bailly
crbailly@bni.com

Dan Georgevich
dang@bni-mi.com

Credits

Developmental Editing: Jeff Morris
Proofreading: Deborah Costenbader, Bobbie Jo Sims
Text Design/Jacket Design/Production: Jeff Morris
Index: Linda Webster

First printing: May 2003

To the tens of thousands of BNI members around the world
and to our families
for their support.

Contents

Acknowledgments

We would like to thank the thousands of business professionals who supported the writing of this book by e-mailing, overnighting, and snail-mailing us their cards. Many responded generously to the request we posted on our website, www.BNI.com, and many others handed us their cards in person during our travels around the globe.

We received more than 2,000 cards from 10 countries:

- United States of America
- United Kingdom
- Canada
- Australia
- New Zealand
- Malaysia
- Singapore
- Ireland
- Sweden
- Barbados

Special thanks go to the many BNI directors and members around the world whose cards make up the major portion of this book.

We are grateful to two excellent proofreaders, Bobbie Jo Sims and Deborah Costenbader, for paying close attention to the errors of our ways, and to Ray Bard for technical assistance in getting this book printed.

The "Good, Fast, Cheap — Pick Any Three" prize goes to Jeff Morris (www.bookmaestro.com), whose editing, design, and layout skills we highly recommend to anyone who wants a good book done on time. This is the fifth book he has done for us, but not the last.

Ivan Misner

Candace Bailly

Dan Georgevich

Thank you to my family, who provide unwavering love and support for my endeavors. Thanks to my girls, Megan and Samantha, for their unconditional love; and to my husband, Donald, for his support and great sense of humor. To Ivan, a special thank you for this incredible opportunity. And to my other fellow coauthor: Good job, Dan. It has been a pleasure and honor to work with you both.

Candace

I want to offer a heartfelt thank you to the BNI Michigan Directors Team, whose hard work and dedication made it possible for me to spend time on this book. Thank you to my parents and my children, who are my inspiration. And a special thank you to Penny Davis for her unwavering support. To Ivan and Candace: It has been a pleasure working with you; writing a book is hard work! And finally, thank you to Ivan for the opportunity to work on this project.

Dan

I would like to thank Beth, Cassie, Trey, and Ashley for their ongoing love, support, and encouragement. I would also like to thank the team at BNI Headquarters who run the ship so well that I can find time to write my books. Finally, I thank my coauthors Dan and Candace. Without their hard work this book would not have been written.

Ivan

About the Authors

Dr. Ivan R. Misner is the founder and CEO of BNI (Business Network Int'l.), the largest business networking organization in the world. Founded in 1985, BNI now has thousands of chapters throughout North America, Europe, Australia, Asia, and Africa. Each year, BNI generates millions of referrals resulting in close to $1 billion worth of business for its members.

Dr. Misner's Ph.D. is from the University of Southern California. He has written five books, including the best-selling *The World's Best Known Marketing Secret* and the *New York Times* bestseller *Masters of Networking*. He is a monthly contributor to the Expert section of Entrepreneur.com and serves on the business administration faculty at Cal Poly University in Pomona, California, as well as the board of directors of the Colorado School of Professional Psychology.

Called the "Networking Guru" by *Entrepreneur* magazine, Dr. Misner is a keynote speaker for major corporations and associations throughout the world. He has been featured in the *Wall Street Journal, Los Angeles Times, New York Times, CEO Magazine,* and numerous TV and radio shows, including CNBC television and the BBC in London. He has twice been nominated for *Inc.* magazine's Entrepreneur of the Year award.

Dr. Misner is on the board of directors of the Haynes Children's Center and is the founder of the BNI Misner Charitable Foundation. He and his wife, Elisabeth, live in Claremont, California, with their three children, Ashley, Cassie, and Trey. In his spare time he is an amateur magician and a black belt in karate.

Candace Bailly began her career as a naval intelligence analyst in the Pentagon; afterward she went on to become the regional director of BNI for the San Diego region and then the executive director for the Oregon and Southwest Washington regions. She opened both of these regions for BNI.

Candace earned her B.S. in Business Administration. She was a contributing author for *Masters of Networking* and has written articles for naval intelligence publications. While with BNI, Candace has served on the cultural diversity committee, planning committees, and the Founders Circle.

Committed to her community, she volunteers her time at her children's school and as a Girl Scout leader for two troops. She is working toward her doctorate degree in psychology and spends her spare time doing yoga and studying.

Candace is married and lives in Sherwood, Oregon with her husband, Donald, and two daughters.

Dan Georgevich has been an executive director for BNI since the mid-'90s, mostly in Michigan. In this role, Dan supports more than 100 BNI chapters, helping business professionals increase their sales. He has spoken to audiences worldwide about the art of building a business by referral. His accomplishments include conducting Certified Networker Program training and doing online interactive sessions on the Internet for international audiences.

Dan has been recognized with national awards for his contributions to helping others get more business through word-of-mouth marketing. He was selected BNI International Director of the Year for 2002 out of more than 500 directors worldwide.

Small but Mighty

1

"**Y**ou don't have it with you?" his colleague asked incredulously. "The most powerful single business tool in the world, one that you had custom-made to fit your needs, a tool that everybody has and wouldn't be caught dead without — you didn't bring yours with you?"

Ivan Misner was chagrined. Yes, he had that tool — hundreds of them, in fact, back at the office — but he had forgotten to bring even one of them with him to the meeting. And he was always telling others to have plenty of them on hand at all times.

Dr. Misner, founder and CEO of BNI (Business Network Int'l.), the world's largest referral networking organization, is fond of telling this story on himself. It shows how much we take for granted and how easily we forget to carry and use this marvelous, compact, energy-efficient, low-cost, low-tech instrument — a self-contained device with no gears, springs, or batteries that keeps working for its owner hours, weeks, years, even decades after it has left his or her hands.

Ivan R. Misner, Ph.D.
Author
Keynote Speaker

199 S. Monte Vista #6
San Dimas, CA 91773-3080
(909) 305-1818 (Inside So. Calif.)
(800) 825-8286 (Outside So. Calif.)
Fax: (909) 305-1811
misner@bni.com

What is this tool?

It's the business card, of course — the most powerful single business tool, dollar for dollar, that you can invest in.

Your business card serves a multitude of functions — none of which go into action *until the second you give it away!*

Benefits

What does your business card do for you?

- It tells people your name and the name of your business.
- It provides your address, telephone number, fax number, e-mail address, website, and other ways of contacting you.
- It lets people know who you are, what you do, what your qualifications are for doing what you do, how the things you do can help them, and perhaps even what you look like.
- It demonstrates in text and graphics why a person should consider doing business with you rather than somebody else.
- It can give others a taste of your work, your style, your personality — even your voice.
- It can persuade the person you give it to that you are intelligent, creative, and resourceful.
- It can be so unusual or attractive or strange or charming or funny that it sticks in the memory like a great radio or television ad.
- It can present the same messages to anybody who gains possession of it, long after it has left your hands for the last time.

The wonders don't stop there. This amazing device

- never needs repair or maintenance,
- requires no license to own or operate,
- can be carried by the dozens in your shirt pocket or purse,
- fits easily and unobtrusively in your hand, and
- starts working automatically the instant you hand it to someone.

Here's the bottom line: this amazing little tool, this tiny advertisement that keeps working and working, is the most cost-efficient promotional device you can own. A simple, elegant, classic business card can lend you and your business an air of quiet professionalism for only a few cents. Splashy, multicolored, attention-grabbing cards can range from dimes to a few dollars.

Yes, you probably already have a business card and use it regularly. But is it effective? Are you getting the full potential from your investment?

Do you know what your card can do and how you can use it for maximum impact?

It helps if you know a little about the history of the business card. Who invented it, and why?

ORIGINS

The modern business card has two ancestral lines, both lost in the mists of history but traceable at least as far back as the 17th century. One bloodline was the calling card or visiting card, used by European aristocrats to communicate with one another and convey social status. The other was the trade card, printed and distributed by merchants to attract customers to their shops.

The social calling card, invented by either the Germans in the 1700s, the French in the 1600s, or the Chinese even earlier (depending on whom you choose to believe), became the basis of elaborate social customs and manners by which the upper classes established and maintained social rank. In 19th-century England, before the telephone was invented, people "came to call" uninvited and offered their card to the butler or maid who answered the door. If the resident was in but not receiving visitors — that is, "not at home" — the caller's card was left in a tray in the entryway. Messages could be conveyed in code; for example, a specific corner of the card could be folded

down to express sympathy, congratulations, or affection. Men and women used different styles of cards and carried them around in cases made of ivory, silver, or papier-maché, depending on the affluence of the owner.

Merchants adapted visiting cards for commercial use, a function that had nothing to do with social rank (people engaged in commerce were considered lower class). Seventeenth-century London was a tough place to do business; transportation was primitive, streets were narrow and congested and filthy, and the city had no coherent street numbering system. To bring in customers, merchants printed cards describing their offerings and including rudimentary maps showing how to get to their front door. Less

expensive printing methods, such as woodcut or letterpress, were used to turn out one-color cards of lower quality than those used by the idle rich, many of whom offered cards displaying fancy calligraphy in color.

Over time, as commerce and the professional middle class grew in size and respectability, businesspeople upgraded the quality of their cards and used them to distinguish their services and products from their competitors'. The fancier and more expensive the card, the higher the class of clientele likely to be attracted. Merchants and tradespeople who had multiple markets or areas or made frequent changes in contact information preferred cheaper, more functional cards.

The use of business cards bloomed in American cities in the 18th century, especially among the most common trades, such as bakers, tailors, and sellers of patent medicine. Copperplate engraving was the state of the art. Paul Revere, the famous horseman and silversmith, produced engraved cards for himself and others.

In the 19th century, business cards began to look more like those of today, with fancy engravings and multicolor lithography. But these were focused mostly on products, not vendors: tobacco, food items, farm equipment, and so forth. Distributed in stores or person-to-person, trade cards were a more economical way of getting the word out than newspaper

ads, which entailed high printing costs.

The dawn of the 20th century brought new technologies that slashed the cost of newspaper and magazine ads. The mass media, starting with radio and exploding into the visual storm of television commercials, caused trade cards to fade from the scene. However, many individuals and businesspeople continued to use visiting cards in one form or another.

As mass-media ads continued to proliferate, however, many business owners felt their message was getting lost in the ever more expensive and crowded airwaves. Meanwhile, printing methods continued to grow in sophistication and affordability. People began to recognize the value of a good business card, and few were those who did not have a Rolodex on their desk. By the end of the millennium, the art of the attractive, eye-catching, yet affordable business card had come into full flower.

FUNCTIONS

The cards you hand to others are like the connectors on a giant networking switchboard. This one connects you with the home builder you just met at the business luncheon; he may refer to it next time he needs an accountant — which could be next week or next year. That one goes to a hair stylist who will stick it in the corner of her salon mirror, where it will be noticed by a real estate agent getting a haircut whose niece is nervous about filling out her first tax return.

These are the two main functions of your card: to gain business from the person you give it to, and to get your name out to other people that first person comes in contact with. It's a low-maintenance way to extend your network in all directions. Wherever your card goes, that's where people take note of you.

You are especially likely to be noticed if (1) your card is passed along by a happy customer, or (2) the card is memorable enough to draw attention to itself and your name. The first situation is something you strive for as a business-person — creating business by being so good, people tell their friends about you. The second circumstance is what this book is about: making your card a powerful networking tool in its own right.

What does an effective business card do?

It defines your identity — that is, it fits your style and personality, and it is appropriate in general for your kind of business and in particular for the ways your business is unique.

It tells people everything they need to know about your products or services, or where they can visit, write, phone, or e-mail to find out more.

Like London's early trade cards, it lets the customer know how to find your place of business.

It's memorable, eye-catching, entertaining, intriguing, engrossing. That is, it keeps you visible. It's the kind of card that people will keep just to look at, even if they think they'll never need your product or service. When it comes time to clean out the old card file, they'll look at yours again and keep it for another year — or perhaps remember it when someone they know needs your product or service.

298 Great Road
PO Box 1285
Littleton, MA 01460
978.952.8880
Fax: 978.952.2622
wisman@ma.ultranet.com

WISMAN
CRONIN
CREATIVE

It stands in for you when you're not around. The only thing some people will know about you is what they can see on the card. If your sparkling personality is instrumental in getting you the kind of customers your business thrives on, make sure that personality comes through on the card when it drifts into the hands of person number 15 next January.

It distinguishes you from your competition, both by emphasizing your specialty and by conveying the quality of your product or service by the quality of your card. If you sell the highest quality furniture in town but your card looks like you spent all of five minutes designing it, you'll get customers who are not prepared to pay your prices while failing to connect with high-dollar prospects.

It's well designed for your market. If your target market is senior citizens, use larger type. If you're a product photographer, put some of your best work on your card. A piano tuner might consider a glossy card with bold black and white design elements; a flower arranger needs lots of color.

It encourages people to seek you out for referral or advice. Your card doesn't have to be a hard sell; let the holder know that you're approachable and friendly, whether or not he wants to buy something. In this way, it becomes a pure networking tool with a longer-lasting value.

As you can see, the modern business card fills just about the same needs as did the 17th-century merchant's trade card and the aristocrat's visiting card — combined.

◆   It tells others who you are and helps you establish your ranking in their world.

- It serves as a record of a visit in person or a contact with a third party you both know, which helps in establishing trust and acceptance.

- It communicates what you do for a living, how your product or service can help the contact, and something of your style of operation.

- It provides practical information on how to get to your address or how to contact you by phone, fax, e-mail, or snail mail.

- It keeps your name in the contact's memory — and the more memorable the card, the longer you stay there.

WHAT'S AHEAD

We've written this book to show you how to make a card that does all of these things very, very well. We've included plenty of examples to teach and inspire you. Some of these will probably give you some great ideas of your own, tricks and techniques you can adapt to your own card to give yourself a head start over your competition.

But before we get into the specifics, we'll spend some time discussing some general principles. You'll learn how to put together a great business card that will set you apart from the crowd and get people to remember you and tell others about you. You'll see how important it is to define yourself clearly and powerfully, and you'll learn the most efficient way of doing this on a 2" x 3½" card. Then we'll talk about different types of cards, their unique characteristics and benefits, and their costs.

Once you're familiar with the elements of business card design, you'll be ready to enjoy and benefit from the heart of the book. Chapters 4 through 12 are filled with dazzling examples to inspire your creativity, ranging from the elegantly simple to the astoundingly imaginative. You'll find yourself coming up with great ideas for giving your own card that extra kick you need to gain an edge over your competition.

After that, we'll go into the practical matter of keeping plenty of cards within reach, as well as where, when, and how to get them into other people's hands. You'll also learn how organizing the cards you receive into a contact database helps you extend and enhance your network. Near the end of the book you'll see a few of the many tools available for producing, organizing and displaying both your own card and the cards of your fellow networkers.

So — what's the secret of powerful marketing and networking? It's in the cards!

Define Yourself

Define Yourself

2

Have you ever tried on an article of "one size fits all" clothing? Didn't fit you all that well, did it? That's why clothing manufacturers make different sizes — and if you want something that's absolutely perfect, you spring for some extra bucks and go to a tailor.

When you're designing your marketing materials, you certainly want them to be tailor-made. Using a generic approach in your ads, brochures, and websites won't set you apart from the crowd; it won't tell people what's distinctive about you, your business, your products or services. It won't cause you to be remembered.

When you advertise your services or products, being specific marks you as an expert. Networkers know that the more you bring your unique personality, needs, and capabilities into your business identity, the more referrals you're likely to receive. The same applies to your marketing materials. To get the kinds of customers you want, good marketing requires you to be specific about what you do and what makes you unique.

A business card is an integral part of a good marketing plan. For its size and cost, it is probably the most powerful part. So it is especially important that your card be one that is memorable and makes a favorable impression. Otherwise, it will probably get tossed into a drawer full of ancient, smudged, forgotten cards that keep accumulating long after the businesses they represent have faded away. That is, if it doesn't get dropped into the nearest circular file.

Your card should display the same design and basic information as your other marketing materials. But a business card is not a brochure or a catalog; space is limited, so you must choose your words and images carefully. Which information is absolutely essential? What else can you include that will help persuade a prospect to contact you? Equally important, what should you leave out? Too much information can dilute or obscure your message.

How do you solve this space-versus-content problem? A good approach is to break the essentials down into three areas: identity, credibility, and clarity. Identity and credibility are concerned with what you should include on your card at a minimum; clarity is more about what to leave off.

IDENTITY

The first step in defining your business self is the "must know" information: Who are you? Where and how can people get in touch with you to avail themselves of your products or services?

Begin creating your business identity by providing the following information on your card:

1. Your name
2. Your title
3. Your department or division
4. The name of your business
5. Your industry or professional specialty
6. Your address
7. Your phone and fax numbers
8. Your e-mail address
9. Your website

These basics can vary, depending on your individual needs. For example, if you do business mainly online, you can make your website URL or e-mail address the most prominent contact information, perhaps even leaving off your telephone number and snail mail address entirely. If you're one of several co-equals in a business, you may choose to display your name less prominently than the name of the business.

So far, you've established that you have a specific name and company and phone number. But that doesn't really say who you are in a personal sense. You could be anybody conducting business at the given location. Exactly what do you do that might cause people to seek you out? Perhaps you're an accountant — but so are thousands of other people. What makes you uniquely qualified to satisfy a customer's unique requirements?

In *The World's Best Known Marketing Secret,* Dr. Misner outlines how to tell people specifically what you do, in the fewest possible words, by breaking down the facts of your business into four basic areas. Using these "lowest common denominators," you establish what is unique about your business:

1. Specific products or services
2. Unique benefits
3. Target markets
4. Professional qualifications

What are your special qualifications, professional and otherwise, for providing your product or service? If you're the exclusive outlet or the patent holder for a highly regarded product, display that fact prominently on your card. If you're the first veterinarian to offer a new, life-saving surgical procedure for dogs, show it on your card. In terms of gaining business and getting the edge over competitors, this may be the most important single bit of information you put on your business card, other than your name.

The same goes for describing unique markets that you serve or any other unique benefits that you provide. Keep your information consistent with the intellectual and interest level of your primary market; answer their most common or likely questions. If your business can be marketed to several groups, consider creating marketing materials specific to each.

You can't be everything to everyone, and neither can a business card. Your card needs to be (1) general enough to encompass most of what your business is about, as well as how to locate or contact you, but (2) specific enough to be distinctly yours, reflecting the uniqueness of your industry, your business, and your target market. Although you'll have to condense your pitch, be sure to keep the look, feel, and message of your business card consistent with the rest of your marketing materials.

CREDIBILITY

Once you've established your basic identity — the who, what, and where of your business and the unique benefits you can provide — the next step is to address the why. Specifically, from the point of view of your prospect: why should she consider doing business with you, rather than with your competitor?

Consumers' buying preferences are influenced by many factors, but the most important factor you can establish with your business card is trust. Just as referrals work because people trust a person or business that has been recommended by a friend or associate, there is information you can put on your card that will gain the trust of a prospect. Below are some kinds of information that will help increase your credibility.

Titles

Showing the name of the position you hold in your company lets clients and prospects know your area of responsibility and makes it easier for them to communicate with you. Titles usually indicate a degree of recognition and accomplishment in your field or company.

Education and credentials

Degrees or certifications tell the prospect you're an expert in your field. It's best to avoid the "alphabet soup" approach ("Susan Smith, BSBA, CNP, IS") and stick to abbreviations that are familiar to the general public, such as PhD, MD, CPA, and RN. Unusual credentials should be spelled out, and should be used only if they augment your credibility with the clients you seek. If you do use an unfamiliar abbreviation, spell it out elsewhere on the card.

Memberships and affiliations

Most industry-specific organizations have strict entry requirements that translate into credibility. Membership in service organizations and other groups also carries extra weight by showing your commitment to the community and knowledge of the value of networking.

Awards and honors

If you or your company have been named to a prestigious list, awarded significant contracts, or honored by an organization in your industry, note it on your card. This adds to your credibility because it indicates that others in your field have recognized your expertise and accomplishments.

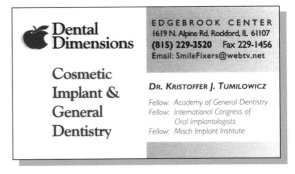

Authorship

If you are a published author, you're considered an expert in your field. Design your card to draw attention to one or more of your book titles.

Years in business

Longevity enhances credibility. If you've been in business for 15 years, or if you work for a 50-year-old company, a prospect will usually have greater confidence in you. However, some companies are viewed more favorably than others. Share this information only if you feel it will genuinely complement your image and community standing.

Schwab Automotive
Your Car Care Specialists

10 Hooke Road, Elizabeth West, South Australia, 5113.
Tel: 08 8252 9333   Fax: 08 8252 9322

Schwab Automotive
Your Car Care Specialists
28 years experience

Automotive Repairs	New vehicle servicing
Tune-ups	Brake & Clutch overhauls
Front suspension repairs	Engine overhauls
Transmission servicing	Cylinder head overhauls
Drive shafts	Cooling systems
Vehicle inspections	Tyre & Wheel balancing

Harlequin Card
(08) 8264 0747   Puncture repairs

Memory hook or tag line

A memory hook is an excellent way of making a good first impression without being there in person. A catchy, creative, engaging phrase or sentence will stay with the prospect longer than any ordinary marketing blurb. In this example, the phrase "We don't mouse around!" works because it is humorous (a pun) and connects with the service offered, which is related to computers. (You can read much more about memory hooks in Dr. Misner's book *Seven Second Marketing*.)

P. Sato
Professional Web Design

"We don't mouse around!"

Paula Sato
909.786.0114
Sato@jurupa.com
www.business-words.com

Philosophy or mission

Describing your philosophy and standards of conducting business can help establish your credentials, especially if your industry encompasses different specialties. A physician, for example, might choose to highlight the use of herbal medicines. Being explicit about your ethical standards can also enhance your credibility.

Not all Accountants are the same!

"Profits give you choices.

Lack of Profits give you no choice at all."

PETER DISNEY A.C.A.
E-MAIL: PeterD@Profit-adviser.co.uk

Founder Member
Association of
Profit Advisers

Contact me at:-

Wood & Disney

THE MANSE
103 HIGH STREET
WIVENHOE
COLCHESTER
ESSEX CO7 9AF
TELEPHONE: (01206) 825447
FACSIMILE: (01206) 827286

Visit us at our Website:
WWW.Profit-adviser.co.uk

OUR PHILOSOPHY

We *recognise, understand and appreciate* that our clients come first.

We *recognise* that our services must make their businesses more successful, enjoyable and secure.

We *understand* our clients' problems, needs, hopes and fears.

We *appreciate* that unless our clients see us as offering them a benefit or advantage they would not do business with us

We aim to achieve this *by looking forward rather than back.*

MISSION STATEMENT

Our mission is to improve the businesses of our clients.
We will achieve this by:-

Providing an exceptional level of care and attention.

Reducing bureaucratic intrusion by offering support in their dealings with all government and regulatory bodies.

Offering assurances that their affairs are dealt with properly and efficiently.

Focusing on proactive forward looking advice.

Identifying opportunities to improve their bottom line potential.

Teaching them to become PROFIT CHAMPIONS.

Not all Accountants are the same!

Wood & Disney

REGISTERED AUDITORS
ACCOUNTANTS &
PROFIT ADVISERS

Convenience

Show the prospect your interest in making her life or business easier by highlighting convenience. How are your products or services more effective or cost efficient than your competitors'? Indicate extended hours of operation, payment options, same-day service, money-back guarantees, free delivery, package rates, and so forth.

GENTLE, EFFECTIVE RELIEF FOR:
Upper and lower body pain • Headaches • Joint pain and muscle spasms • Stress-related discomfort • Sports, workplace, and personal injuries • Chronic pain • Pregnancy-related back pain

WE OFFER:
Nutrition counseling • Individualized treatment recommendations Gentle therapeutic adjustments • Deep-tissue work • Massage therapy • Same-day appointments, evening hours • Convenient location • Flexible payment options

Member:
International Chiropractic Assoc.
American Chiropractic Association
Chiropractic Association of Oregon
Palmer College of Chiropractic Alumni Assoc.

912 Main Street • Oregon City, Oregon 97045

Fax (503) 722-3938
(503) 656-1415

JENNIFER L. PITCAIRN, D.C.

CLARITY

The information described above can amount to a pretty good chunk of print to be squeezed into a sliver of paper two inches by three-and-a-half, even if you use both sides. But this is essential information, and it can usually be composed in an eye-pleasing and user-friendly arrangement that will bring you attention and business.

In fact, you can usually include more information than the minimum, if you use the space efficiently or if you use a nonstandard or oversized format. But the danger, even working within a larger area, is that you can include so many words, logos, pictures, and graphic elements that your message gets lost in the clutter.

An entrepreneur we know bought out an automotive service business that included a repair shop and a car wash. The property was a mess: broken-down cars parked out by the curb, a rusty cyclone fence, no landscaping. A weathered sign on the lot and another on the company truck listed various repair services; a smaller, inconspicuous sign on the building advertised the car wash.

The new owner wanted to get more customers into his car wash, thinking this would increase his repair business as well. But when he looked at his own shop from the street, he could see what he was up against. The front of the building, where the shiny, freshly washed cars were parked, could not be seen from the road. Between the signs and the clutter, it was hard to tell exactly what was going on behind the chain-link fence.

He quickly set about changing things to make the car wash visible from the road. He moved the vehicles awaiting repair, along with the repair truck, out of sight behind the building. He took down the fence and gave the building a new paint job. He landscaped the grounds with grass and low shrubs.

The most effective thing he did, though, was replace the signs. Instead of the jumbled listing of services on scattered signs, his two new signs, high on a pole in the middle of his new front yard, read simply:

Car Wash

Vehicle Repair

The newly refurbished business soon began attracting new customers. Many drive-bys who pulled in for the first time remarked that they had never realized this was a car wash.

The same principle applies to all marketing materials, especially your business card. As you design your card, think like the master sculptor Michelangelo, who envisioned his masterpiece inside a block of marble and simply carved away everything that wasn't part of it. Don't try to cram in a laundry list of every possible product or service you offer. You want your message to come across at a glance. Narrow it down to the one or two most significant items.

Equally important, as you'll see in the next chapter, avoid visual clutter. Make sure the overall appearance of the card enhances your message rather than obscuring it. Make it so pleasing that people will enjoy looking at it — and keep it.

Design
Your
Card

3

Once you've defined your business self by providing basic information and credentials, the next task is to build a card on this foundation — to flesh it out in a way that is unique, informative, appropriate to your business image, and memorable. Your goal should be to have a card that accurately represents the products or services you offer, gives your business a positive image, and is memorable. Ultimately, you want your contact to do four things:

1. Keep your card
2. Remember you
3. Contact you
4. Refer you to others

The word "memorable" is important. You want your card to be one that invites a second glance and doesn't get tossed in a dusty drawer. You want it to be a card that makes a person smile and share; a card that comes immediately to mind when he or someone he knows needs a service or product like yours. In marketing, memorable is a good thing to be.

YOUR "LOOK"

When you first notice a business card that leaves an indelible impression on you, the thing that catches your attention is almost always the way it looks, rather than the words. This doesn't necessarily mean the card is flashy or colorful; sometimes it's the pure, elegant simplicity of a classic design that invites admiration and closer scrutiny. Whatever the design, though, it's important for the look of your card to be coordinated with the rest of your marketing materials and to reflect the image and identity of your company or business.

The kind of business card you use should depend primarily on your target market. Know what approach to take. A simple, classic card may not have the impact needed for some professions; a full-color card with pictures may be too flashy for others. We know many people who use different cards for different target markets. You wouldn't think twice about running different ads for different markets; the same should apply to your cards.

- ◆ For doctors, lawyers, financial planners, and other specialties involving serious life or business issues, a conservative look is usually most appropriate.

- ◆ An architect or graphic designer needs a more dramatic and eye-catching card that expresses creativity and design sense.

- ◆ A high-tech company might go for an engineered look, perhaps even one of the new wave of multimedia CD cards.

- ◆ Businesses whose typical customers are people in their middle years or older are wise to use larger type and a less flashy design.

Whatever the boundaries pushed, good design rests on a foundation of well-established design principles, such as the importance of open space. Music lovers understand that some of the breaks between notes are as important as the notes themselves. Actors speaking lines know the impact of a well-placed pause. The graphic design analog, "white space," is empty space that separates and highlights significant information and leads the reader's eye from one point to another. White space is key to reducing clutter and keeping your message clear.

Guidelines are sometimes violated successfully, because taste is subjective and relative. A card that one person might consider downright gaudy may attract exactly the sort of attention another business owner seeks. A classic card that appeals to conservative personalities may seem unbearably stuffy and boring to a more adventurous soul. Whatever your approach, avoid a cluttered or overstuffed look. Too much information is counterproductive; anything that doesn't help build a clear picture of you and your business only gets in the way.

The most important guideline is integrity; keep the card, as well as your entire marketing package, consistent with your business identity and personal style. Consider how it will look to Joe Stranger. What kind of first impression does it make? Is this the way you want to be perceived by someone you've never met?

Based on these and other design principles, we can divide cards into several general styles. Each of these types is discussed below, along with an example illustrating the design elements involved.

STYLE

Choose a card style that's appropriate for your business, your industry, and your personal style. If you're a funeral director, you don't want to be caught handing out day-glo cards with cartoon figures on them. If you're a mechanic whose specialty is converting old Beetles into dune buggies, a formal, black-on-white engraved card will probably be dropped into the nearest circular file. Start with the style that best supports the business image you wish to project.

Basic cards

This is a good card style when utility is all you need. It's a no-nonsense approach that can appeal to clients and prospects who would not be impressed by fancy design features — the people who want "just the facts,

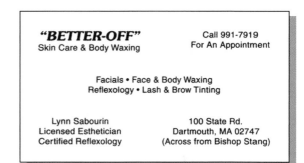

ma'am." The design is simple, the information clear and concise. A basic card is usually printed in black ink on plain white or cream stock.

Classic cards

The classic style is a more image-conscious design than the basic. Based on the historical origins of social calling cards, it's simple but elegant, with more attention paid to type-face, layout, and graphic elements. Classic cards often use fancier type styles, such as calligraphic script, and are more likely to include elements such as a logo or other simple graphic with a touch of color.

Splash cards

One popular type of business card is essentially a classic card with a

multicolor splash — more than just the logo, and a lot more eye-catching than the classic, but using basic classic layout and typography. It's a tasteful way to catch the prospect's eye without overpowering your basic information.

Picture cards

Having your face on your card helps a contact remember you the next

time she sees you, whether it's a photograph, a drawing, or a caricature. Images representing a product or service, or a benefit your business provides, can help you communicate your business better than dozens of words. Color is often helpful on a picture card.

Full-color cards

The boldest use of color occurs on full-color cards, which are often

printed on bright colored stock using four-color process, metallic inks, or other color devices. Both sides typically take advantage of the full range of colors.

Tactile cards

Some cards are distinguished not so much by how they look as by how they feel. They may use nonstandard materials, such as metal or wood, or have unusual shapes, edges, folds, or embossing. Tactile cards tend to be considerably more expensive than regular cards because they use nonstandard production processes such as die cuts.

Multipurpose cards

A card can do more than promote your name and business — it can also serve as a discount coupon, an appointment reminder, or for some other function. A card of any type can be made multipurpose.

The secret of successful media coverage is not just writing a good press release but knowing how to get it published.

Customer Guarantee

Your first press release will be *FREE* if we fail to get it published.

Contact us on 01767 601470 for full details.

ULTIMEDIA
MARKETING LIMITED

We met on

....

at ....

and discussed

call me on ....

"Overnight we had the resources of an experienced and professional team carrying out public relations, marketing and promotional activities which fully support the aims of our sales department"
David McGee
Fibre Optech Ltd

"Since we appointed Ultimedia, our average weekly sales enquiries have increased by over 20%"
Tony Hacker
Endoline Machinery

"I would gladly sell my house and children for the benefit of Ultimedia - they are that good!"
Paul Beasley ACII
RHG Corporate Insurance Group

Series and collection cards

If your business needs to wear different faces for different markets,

you may need a series of cards to reflect these differences. The basic information and look is usually similar, but with variations for different audiences. Some series cards are designed to become collectibles.

Outside-the-box cards

A wildly original, fanciful, or extravagant presentation can draw extra attention. Creativity knows no bounds — except the amount of money you wish to spend, which we've saved to discuss last.

Cost

After you have read and enjoyed the next nine chapters, you should have a pretty good idea of the approach you want to take on your next business card. But there's one other consideration, and it's not a trivial one: how much will it cost?

A business card is perhaps the most cost-effective marketing tool you can own. But it's not chump change, and when any important information changes — address or telephone number, for example — you should toss out whatever cards you have left and print another batch. It is true that reprinting, even with minor text changes, is usually less expensive than the first run of a new design. But a card with multiple colors, nonstandard size or folds, die cuts, or other unusual design features will always be more expensive than a simpler card for any given quantity.

Any card based on a standard design or template can save you the cost of commissioning an original or personalized design. If you work in a company that uses a standardized card, your costs (and design decisions) will be less. If you own your own business or work for one that is creative in nature (such as a graphic design or public relations firm), you might use multicolored or high-concept cards, or possibly have a range of designs to choose from. You can expect to shell out more money if you avail yourself of the services of a good graphic designer.

Other than design, what factors control the cost? There are several, most of them design-dependent.

- ◆ Quantity. The more you print of a given design, the lower your unit cost.
- ◆ Quality of stock. Colored or textured materials cost more than plain white card stock, and exotic materials such as plastic, wood, or metal can be much more expensive.
- ◆ Number of inks. Printing in one color is least expensive; two-color printing costs more than twice as much. Expenses increase with each additional ink, but full color using the four-color process (cyan, magenta, yellow, and black inks) often costs little more than two or three colors, depending on the press type. High-resolution, full-color, photo-quality printing costs about three times as much as one-color printing.

Other factors can raise costs in minor or major ways:

- ◆ Sizes or proportions different from standard, especially larger.
- ◆ Printing on both sides.

- Bleeds (printing all the way to the edge of the card).
- Folding, as with brochure-type cards.
- Embossing (raised letters or shapes).
- Specialty inks, foils, coatings, or other applied materials.
- Die cuts, lamination, gluing, and other special procedures.

Costs vary from printer to printer, and new technologies, such as digital printing, are continually stirring the competitive stew. But if you ask for bids from several printers, you can usually find an affordable way to produce the card you want. Compare traditional printers, large office supply stores, copy shops, quick-print shops, and companies that specialize in business cards. Many attractive designs can be ordered over the Internet, and the job cost may be lower if you let the supplier put his imprint on the back. If you're the do-it-yourself type, you can save a ton of money on a simple card by designing and printing out cards using your computer.

Be flexible with your specifications; sometimes you can save a great deal by making a few small changes in design, format, ink type, or other specification. Ask the printer what materials she has in stock that she needs to unload. She may cut you a terrific bargain. Ask about printing on material that's available to your business at low cost, such as wood veneer, leather, or metal. See if you can get a lower quote by allowing the printer more time to complete the job.

The
Basic
Card

The
Basic
Card

4

Straightforward and simple, the basic card carries only essential information. Its format is plain and uncluttered, usually containing text only, but sometimes including a logo, or perhaps a simple graphic, such as a line, to offset or highlight important information. Beyond making it look clean and coherent, little time or effort is spent on design.

Two kinds of businesses typically use basic cards:

Conservative. In many professions, especially those dealing with serious life issues such as health, money, and legal problems, it is considered a liability to come across as flashy or artsy. The simple look and low-key presentation of the basic card communicates reserve, respect, and reliability.

New. For a startup company, the basic card is a fast, low-cost way to get the word out and plant the seeds for a broad network of customers, prospects, and contacts. When executed well, the basic card gives an image of straight-talking action and effectiveness that communicates the vitality of a young but growing business.

Hallmarks of the typical basic card are

- Clean layout
- Text and little else
- One or two type styles
- Few or no graphic elements
- Standard size
- Landscape (horizontal) format

- ◆ One color only, typically black
- ◆ Printing on one side only, without bleeds

There are exceptions to these characteristics, but in general, the basic card is an inexpensive, low-key, tasteful way to promote your business or profession. The following examples show many of the ways businesses and individuals use this type of card.

Profession: Attorney
Name: Christopher T. Hildebrandt
Company: Richards and Kelly
Country: USA

On this two-sided basic card, all the essential contact information is on the front; location, specialties, and other information are on the back. It's printed in one color — blue — and shows a little more than minimal design values. But it's simple and low in cost.

It's a keeper because:
- ◆ Simple graphics add energy to the design
- ◆ Nonstandard fonts are unusual but not flamboyant
- ◆ Profession stands out at top

> ### Attorney
>
> A General Law Practice Concentrating In:
> ### Medical Malpractice
> ### Personal Injury
>
> *Richards & Kelly*
> 429 Fourth Avenue - 900 Law & Finance Building
> Pittsburgh, PA 15219
>
> Free Initial Consultation

"BETTER-OFF"
Skin Care & Body Waxing

Call 991-7919
For An Appointment

Facials • Face & Body Waxing
Reflexology • Lash & Brow Tinting

Lynn Sabourin
Licensed Esthetician
Certified Reflexology

100 State Rd.
Dartmouth, MA 02747
(Across from Bishop Stang)

Profession: Skin care & body waxing
Name: Lynn Sabourin
Company: Better Off
Country: USA

With its symmetrically balanced design, this card establishes credibility by showing license and certification, gives location landmarks, and makes it clear that appointments are required.

It's a keeper because:

◆ Symmetrical design is clean and balanced
◆ Services are well defined
◆ Credibility is established
◆ Landmark gives location

Profession: Solicitor
Name: Rhodri Rees
Company: Adams Harrison
Country: UK

This card is clean and neat, with emphasis on the name of the contact. The cream-colored stock and black type make this a good example of the basic style, but the colored graphic line takes it to the next level.

It's a keeper because:

◆ Graphic line in contrasting color adds visual interest
◆ Contact name is prominent
◆ Identification of contact as partner lends credibility

Adams
Harrison *Solicitors*

Rhodri Rees
Partner

52a High Street, Haverhill, Suffolk, CB9 8AR
Tel: (01440) 702485 Fax: (01440) 706820 Dx: 80350 Haverhill

B.E. Rachman
Attorney At Law

(760) 720-9324 Office
(760) 850-1045 Pager
(760) 729-2429 Fax
e.mail: belindaesq@hotmail.com

800 Grand Avenue, Suite. A-21, Carlsbad, California 92008

Profession: Attorney
Name: B. E. Rachman
Company: B. E. Rachman,
Country: USA

This is a good example of a basic card that uses minimal graphics (the box) to highlight the name of the firm. The bold text leads the eye to the all-important contact information.

It's a keeper because:

◆ Fonts are crisp, easy to read
◆ Text groupings contribute to integrity of design
◆ Black-on-white design is used to maximum advantage

Profession: Sales & training consultant
Name: Stuart Coleman
Company: Hollycomms Direct Ltd
Country: UK

This basic card is all text, even the logo. The interlaced "HC" in the upper left corner attracts the eye and helps in locating the card in a book or Rolodex. All the information that's needed for an effective business presentation is here.

Stuart Coleman
Sales & Training Consultant

Hollycomms Direct Ltd
21 Brybank Road
Haverhill
Suffolk CB9 7WD
Telephone: 0870 730 7300

It's a keeper because:

◆ It's a no-nonsense card
◆ All essential information is present
◆ Large type is user-friendly

Profession: Attorney
Name: SusAnne Lee Jenkins
Company: SusAnne Lee Jenkins
Country: USA

In a multicultural community, being bilingual is an asset. This card has the same information on both sides but in different languages. The boxed quote is a key to Ms. Jenkins's code of ethics, and the license numbers add more credibility.

It's a keeper because:

◆ Contact information is grouped, easy to read
◆ Availability of services across cultures is highlighted
◆ Textured tan card stock lends distinction to simple basic design

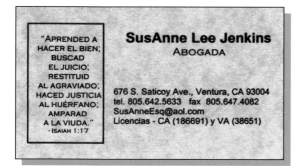

Profession: Interior design
Name: Amir A. Ghavami
Company: The Interior Design Center, Inc.
Country: USA

In a subdued, tasteful way, this basic card displays flair and creativity — essential information for the profession represented.

It's a keeper because:

◆ Layout is balanced, pleasing
◆ Sense of design is apparent
◆ Navy blue type on white card stock is clean and classy

The Interior Design Center, Inc.

Amir A. Ghavami
License # 728793

818•342•0044
818•342•0217 fax

19218 Ventura Blvd.
Tarzana, CA 91356

Robin Schuckmann
Desktop Publisher & Technical Editor

Print Media Solutions
12755 SW Marie Court
Tigard, OR 97223

Phone: 503-590-9575
Fax: 305-422-0191
zonich@cyberhighway.net

Profession: Desktop publishing
Name: Robin Schuckmann
Company: Print Media Solutions
Country: USA

Desktop publishing requires the ability to communicate vital information in a visually pleasing graphic design. This card succinctly demonstrates the business owner's marketable skills.

It's a keeper because:

◆ Balanced, symmetrical layout demonstrates owner's design skills
◆ Fonts are compatible, crisp, easy to read
◆ Dark blue type on off-white stock is clean, stylish

Profession: Dentistry
Name: Charlene Gale
Company: Gilbert H. Snow, DDS, Inc
Country: USA

Subtle cues, such as the bright white card stock and the unobtrusive snowflakes, tie the design of this basic card to the business name (Dr. Snow) and the profession (think clean white teeth). The whole card acts as a memory hook.

It's a keeper because:

◆ Layout is balanced and visually pleasing
◆ Stock and ink colors carry through on a theme
◆ Crucial information stands out

Profession: Web design
Name: Ben McKinley
Company: Mt Hood Software
Country: USA

Both the simplicity and the assymmetrical layout of this card communicate the cutting-edge nature of this high-tech profession. All contact information is easy to read, and the motto provides a reason to use it.

It's a keeper because:
- Simplicity befits high-tech profession
- Motto lends credibility
- It's easy to read

Profession: Accounting
Name: David C. Murray
Company: Murray Wells Wendeln & Robinson CPAs, Inc
Country: USA

The company's boxed logo, upper left corner, serves as a visual cue when looking for this card. The two inks used contrast attractively and make this basic card stand out.

It's a keeper because:
- Logo placement makes card easy to find
- All company information is easy to read
- Horizontal lines lead eye to company and individual names

M	W
W	R

David C. Murray, CPA
Manager
davem@mwwr.net

Murray Wells
Wendeln & Robinson CPAs, Inc.
Certified Public Accountants • Advisors

121 W. Franklin St. • P.O. Box 403 • Troy, Ohio 45373-0403
937.335.6374 • Fax 937.335.8299 • www.mwwr.net

蕭 玉 鳳 文學士
Seow Gek Hong B.A.
Director

BIM

**BUSINESS & INDUSTRIAL MANAGEMENT
CONSULTANTS (M) SDN. BHD.** (Co. No. 24408-A)

工 商 管 理 顧 問 (馬) 有 限 公 司

秘書，組織有限公司及管理服務。
Secretarial, company incorporation and management services.
Unit 901, Level 9, City Plaza
No. 21, Jalan Tebrau, 80300 Johor Bahru, Johor, Malaysia.
Tel: 607-3331898, 3312899 & 3356898 Fax: 607-3330899
E-mail: bimc@po.jaring.my

Profession: Management
consulting
Name: Seow Gek Hong
Company: BiM
Country: Malaysia

When your target market speaks a different language, your marketing materials need to be bilingual to get the message across — and that includes your business card. This basic card is a good example of intercultural marketing savvy.

It's a keeper because:

◆ It's bilingual
◆ It's simple and functional
◆ All essential information is available at a glance
◆ Logo in bright color attracts attention

The
Classic
Card

5

In the same way that a classic car is a refinement of the basic automobile, the classic card takes the essential simplicity of the basic card and heightens the impact by judiciously augmenting and elaborating its features. The virtues of the basic card — uncluttered, tasteful, reserved, with simple graphics and plenty of white space — are retained, but with more sophisticated design values. The result is a more polished, confident presentation with an aura of wisdom and experience.

In general, a classic card differs from a basic card in several ways:

- ◆ More expensive materials
- ◆ More complicated printing techniques
- ◆ Different formatting and layout
- ◆ More fonts, graphics, and creative elements

A classic card at the conservative end of the spectrum can look very much like a basic card, but a closer inspection is likely to reveal significant differences: higher-quality card stock, letterpress or intaglio printing, more complex graphics, more distinguished typefaces, printing on both sides of the card, perhaps a portrait (vertical) orientation. At the other extreme, classic cards push the boundaries with colored stock, bolder ink colors and combinations, bleeds, unusual fonts, and more creative graphics.

The broader range of elements used in the classic style allow you to express your individuality and command respect without overstating your case or pushing the boundaries of good taste. The essential information is there, as is the basic simplicity of design and materials, but a new dimension is added. A classic card is more likely to stand out and be recognized in a business card book or Rolodex.

Classic cards are often the choice of large, established companies. To maintain a consistent corporate image and yet allow for individual preferences, many companies offer a selection of standard formats with a common theme. To project a similar aura of size and success, many smaller companies and operations also find the classic style a good fit. The classic style is often the second card style chosen by a startup company once it is up and running.

Printing costs for classic cards are generally higher than basic, but still reasonable.

Profession: Menswear
Name: Steven R. Laughlin
Company: Laughlin's Menswear
Country: USA

It's a keeper because:

- Weight and color of card stock fit image of masculine elegance
- Use of "white space" highlights design and text elements
- Font choice speaks to high-end clientele

The antique font on the front of its card gives this business a formal, conservative, high-end image. The heavy, tweedy brown card stock evokes the weight and feel of high-quality clothing. A map on the back harks back to the original purpose of trade cards in old London.

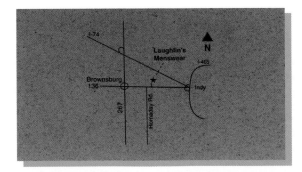

Stephen J. Walsh   President

STEPHEN J.
WAL/H
ELECTRIC, INC.

Phone (617) 859-4500   License #A15143
Fax (781) 335-1680   P.O. Box 303
Pager (617) 465-9735   Weymouth, MA 02190

Profession: Electrician
Name: Stephen J. Walsh
Company: Stephen J. Walsh
Electric, Inc.
Country: USA

Tying the cardholder's name to his industry is a visual pun, the lightning-bolt "S" in the logo, whose vivid color strengthens the memory hook. The credibility that comes from the title at upper right is further enhanced by including the owner's operating license number.

It's a keeper because:

- ◆ Classical symmetry adds balance
- ◆ Logo's vivid visual pun sticks in memory
- ◆ License number adds credibility

Profession: Accounting
Name: Eamonn Leahy
Company: Leahy & Co
Country: Ireland

This is a good example of the clean, classic look in a portrait format. The muted tones of the design elements at the top draw the eye to the company name and motto; contact information is found directly below in a centered text block framed by white space.

It's a keeper because:

- ◆ Classic look works in portrait format
- ◆ Understated design fits industry image
- ◆ Motto states pride in customer satisfaction

LE&HY
CO

Clients Recommend Us

CHARTERED ACCOUNTANTS

Eamonn Leahy
F.C.A. A.I.T.I.

Registered Auditors,
70 Amiens Street,
Dublin 1.
Tel: (01) 855 5100
Fax: (01) 836 5609
Email: leahyco@iol.ie

Profession: Executive search
Name: Philip de Belder
Company: de Belder Associates
Country: UK

This card uses two inks in different screen densities, giving a subdued feeling of extra color, but with dignity. An unobtrusive but integral part of the design, the large, light-gray background text provides important information about the company's services.

It's a keeper because:

◆ Subdued color supports conservative image

◆ Design is clean, modern

◆ Info on company's services is highlighted as design element

---

Profession: Photography
Name: Rebecca Masland
Company: Seize the Moment!
Country: USA

Here is a logo showing action caught in a moment of time — the way a photograph can "seize the moment." Black and red inks on fiber-flecked tan stock create a look that is lively but not gaudy.

It's a keeper because:

◆ Layout and colors are eye-catching, attractive

◆ Logo is highly appropriate for profession, company name

◆ Essential information is easy to read

ST GEORGE & ASSOCIATES
CHARTERED ACCOUNTANTS

Principal
Geraldine St George B.COM., F.C.A., F.C.I.S.

Suite 5, 36 Belmore St, Burwood N.S.W. 2134
PO Box 422, Burwood N.S.W. 1805
Tel: (02) 9715 2122   Fax: (02) 9715 2125
Mobile: 0414 536 234
Email: stgeorge&associates@stga.com.au

Web: www.stga.com.au

Profession: Accounting
Name: Geraldine St. George
Company: St. George & Associates Chartered Accountants
Country: Australia

The owner's signature on one end of the card serves as a logo and an implicit personal guarantee of service. The company's philosophy, on the back of the card, further reinforces credibility.

It's a keeper because:

◆ Vertical bar adds interest to landscape format
◆ Signature, motto lend credibility
◆ Colored block, lines highlight contact info

the **approach** to:

Our **work** is ......
    detailed, reliable & thorough

Our **advice** is ......
    informative, educational & complete

Profession: Management consulting
Name: Louise Beauchamp
Company: Hanchett Consultants Limited
Country: UK

Dark blue ink on smooth white stock are a good fit for a firm specializing in corporate consulting. The red in the logo makes the company's name stand out in the "H" section of the Rolodex.

It's a keeper because:

◆ Presentation is reserved, tasteful
◆ Basic contact info is easy to read
◆ Logo placement gets attention

HANCHETT CONSULTANTS LIMITED

Louise Beauchamp

Tel/Fax: 01440 703959
Mobile: 07787 935664
email: hanchet@dial.pipex.com

For all your ISO 9000 requirements

Profession: Manicure
Name: Sa-ree
Company: BeauImáge Salon and Day Spa
Country: USA

This is an excellent example of a portrait-formatted classic card with a sophisticated look. The company descriptor in colored script gives a personal touch, while the clean, sans serif typeface and color accent below blend well with the off-white, matte-finish card stock.

It's a keeper because:

◆ Crisp, elegant look speaks to high-end customers
◆ Warm colors are attractive, friendly
◆ Plenty of white space sets off contact information

Profession: Graphic design
Name: Sandi Ballard
Company: Visual Communication Design Studio
Country: USA

This card shows off the studio's design capabilities and sensibilities. The Egyptian cartouche alludes to the tradition of visual communication, and the motto beneath spells out the owner's philosophy. Gold foil on the logo and accents blend well with the burgundy type and natural card stock.

It's a keeper because:

◆ Portrait layout echoes logo shape
◆ Card stock and ink colors express sophisticated design values
◆ Message demonstrates company's work and gives contact information

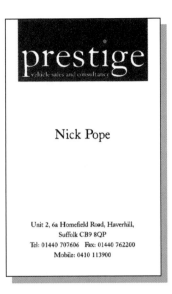

Profession: Sales
Name: Nick Pope
Company: Prestige Vehicle Sales and Consultancy
Country: UK

This elegantly simple card is designed to attract high-end automobile buyers. The principle ink color is close to British Racing Green, a classic automobile color; the single accent in red draws the eye to the company name.

It's a keeper because:

◆ Elegant design is aimed at high-dollar customers
◆ White space is used effectively to highlight name
◆ Second color is used minimally but effectively

Profession: Club manager
Name: Larry B. Ahlquist
Company: City Club
Country: USA

A classic in every way, this card uses a clean design and subdued color to create a feeling of calm and order. The use of a second language on the back of the card directly addresses this club's multicultural target market.

L A R R Y   B .   A H L Q U I S T
General Manager

333 South Grand Avenue
54th Floor, Wells Fargo Center
Los Angeles, California 90071
Telephone 213-620-9662
Fax 213-620-0895
larry.ahlquist@ourclub.com
www.icityclub.com

CITY CLUB

ON BUNKER HILL

It's a keeper because:

◆ Clean design creates upscale market image
◆ Bilingual appeal targets broader client base
◆ Contact information is easy to read

シティ・クラブ・オン・バンカーヒル

ラリー・アルクィスト

ジェネラル マネージャー

カリフォルニア州ロサンゼルス市 サウス・グラント通り 333
ウエルズ ファルゴ センター =5450
電話 (213) 620-9662

Profession: Executive concierge
Name: Blair Smith
Company: Buying Time
Country: USA

This is a bold, modernistic approach to the classic card. The company name and motif on the front allude to the value of time to the executive; the manager's name and contact information are attractively presented in a standard typeface on the reverse.

It's a keeper because:

◆ Graphic is a perfect tie-in with company name and service

◆ Company name with casual, handwritten look alludes to rushed, crowded workday

◆ Information is uncrowded, easy to read

6035 north seventeenth street
phoenix, arizona 85016

blair smith
manager

tel 602 264 5811
fax 602 234 1103
blair@buyingtimeaz.com
www.buyingtimeaz.com

The Splash Card

6

Some cards include a spot or "splash" of color that is designed to catch the eye and make the card stand out in a crowd of more conventional cards. The splash card is essentially a classic card with either an unusually colorful or fanciful logo or a bright color graphic added that is not essential information.

A splash card works by drawing attention irresistibly to the artwork. If it works well, a person may spend a few minutes studying and admiring it, perhaps passing it around and commenting on it. It's the kind of card people are likely to keep, to look at again and again, and to remember when a need arises for your products or services.

A typical splash card

◆ Builds on a classic card design

◆ Uses a standard card size and format

◆ Displays bright colors, unusual fonts, and distinctive artwork

Adding a splash of color is not a good do-it-yourself exercise. It's too easy to produce a colorful card that appears cheap and amateurish, a look that is not likely to build a prospect's confidence in your professional standards. Hire a good graphic designer who can help you come up with an attractive and creative card. Even if you already have a professionally designed logo, you'll need an expert's eye to integrate it into your card effectively. A really bad-looking card can easily be produced by dropping a slick, colorful logo onto a card that looks like it came off a typewriter.

In general, adding bright color elements to a classic card does not raise the cost substantially over that of an ordinary two-color card. Unless the design includes unusual materials, bleeds, or double-sided printing, a splash card can be one of the most economically effective cards you can use. It will give you an immediate edge over your competitors, the ones who hand out that expensive but plain-looking specimen.

Premium Seats For...
CONCERTS · SPORTS · THEATRE

Scott Herbert

P.925-838-0193 • F.925-838-8783
1-800-367-8499
2410 SAN RAMON VALLEY BLVD. • SUITE 250
SAN RAMON, CA 94583
WWW.JUSTTIX.COM

Profession: Ticket sales
Name: Scott Herbert
Company: Just Tix
Country: USA

This glossy card with its bright, colorful cartoon looks sporty — which befits the business of selling premium tickets to sports and other entertainment events. Important contact numbers are highlighted, and on the reverse are listed some of the teams and events covered.

49ERS
RAIDERS
WARRIORS
KINGS
SHARKS
GIANTS
A'S
THEATRE
CONCERTS
WORLD SERIES
SUPERBOWL
FINAL FOUR
NBA FINALS
STANLEY CUP
ALL STAR GAMES
US OPEN * WIMBLEDON
LOCAL AND NATIONAL EVENTS

It's a keeper because:
◆ Sans serif font makes for clean, dynamic look
◆ Colorful artwork demands attention
◆ Listing on reverse gives specific reasons to call

Profession: Cosmetic tattooing
Name: Liz Prom
Company: Beauty is Skin Deep
Country: USA

The color on this card both catches the eye and portrays the service rendered. The use of script and standard fonts to distinguish creative from practical information is effective.

It's a keeper because:

◆ Eye is drawn to swirling patterns around face

◆ Fancy script suggests artistry

◆ Use of credentials helps create confidence

Profession: Magician
Name: Philip A. Smith
Company: Abracadabra Productions
Country: USA

The splash of color on this magician's card is the stylized brim of the hat with a rabbit popping out of it. On a simple white card with standard black type, this color pops out more vividly than full-color images on more lavishly produced cards.

It's a keeper because:

◆ Simple design keeps costs low

◆ Shiny red swatch grabs the eye

◆ Graphic treatment fits the profession

Profession: Chiropractic
Name: Bryan Baisinger
Company: Clearwater Chiro-
practic & Massage
Country: USA

The design of this colorful logo contains several hidden messages. The rippled lines and edges — universal symbols for water (as in "Clearwater") — and the flexible figure echo the purpose of chiropractic: fluidity of movement, by day and by night.

It's a keeper because:

♦ Colorful logo contains strong message about massage
♦ Text is printed in logo colors
♦ Vital info is easy to read

Profession: Graphic design
Name: Lois Wisman
Company: Wisman Cronin Creative
Country: USA

The bright colors and simple geometric shapes of the logo immediately cue the reader to the graphic skills of the company. Offsetting most of the "weight" to the top of the card lends an edginess that communicates creativity.

It's a keeper because:

♦ Fiber-fleck card stock gives casual feel
♦ Avant-garde design demonstrates firm's sense of style
♦ Script signature personalizes the card

Profession: Interior design
Name: Sue Elmange
Company: Sue Elmange
Design Center
Country: USA

INTERIOR DESIGNER
925 Regal Canyon Drive • Walnut, California 91789
(909) 595-5558

This card defines the term "splash." Vivid blotches of color, as on an artist's palette, highlight the handwritten name and tell of the firm's creative spirit. The title and contact elements are simple and clear.

It's a keeper because:

◆ Color swatch draws attention directly to owner's name

◆ Composition is symmetrical and formal, yet feels casual

◆ All information is clear and easily readable

Profession: Answering service
Name: Celia Strother
Company: Answering Service, Inc.
Country: USA

The bright color graphic on this card serves triple duty. It attracts the eye; it names the company; and the "I" represents a person talking on the telephone. The flush-right contact information gives the card a pleasing overall balance.

It's a keeper because:

◆ Colorful logo serves triple duty

◆ Contact information is well-grouped

◆ Plenty of white space helps logo stand out

Celia Strother
Sales Coordinator

25140 Lahser
Suite 121
Southfield, MI 48034

248-353-2234
800-686-3020
Fax: 248-358-3502

Answering Service, Inc.
The Telemessaging Specialists

Profession: Home appraisal
Name: Carol Gronseth
Company: Spectrum Systems, Inc.
Country: USA

The splash in this color-framed card depicts a structure developing from blueprint into finished home — an architectural representation of the appraisal company's start-to-finish involvement.

It's a keeper because:

◆ Rectilinear drawing harmonizes with card shape
◆ Bright blue background stands out in a box of neutral-colored cards
◆ Profession is clearly defined in words and graphics

Profession: Embroidery
Name: Nancy Hart
Company: Hart Design
Country: USA

The soft, red logo ties the owner's name to her craft. The second, deeper-red heart and the thread lead the eye to contact information; the logo is even integrated in miniature with the text. The use of a font resembling hand printing completes the image of skilled handwork.

It's a keeper because:

◆ Harmony of name, color, logos, and font gives design integrity
◆ Placement of elements leads eye to contact information
◆ It's distinctive and memorable

Profession: Technical writing
Name: David Williams
Company: Idea Engineers
Country: USA

In this compelling two-color design, the contact information stands out because of its unusual slant. The logo at left seems to mesh with the rack across the top that highlights a memory hook. The image of engineering words to fit technical specifications is echoed by the simple motto on the reverse.

It's a keeper because:

◆ Logo and layout carry the technical theme

◆ Black and yellow color combo is bold but not overwhelming

◆ Empty space is used effectively

Bobbie Jo Sims
Piano Coach

"Light your creative spark."

1906 Vincent Street
Brownwood, Texas 76801

Phone: 915/641-0224
bj9@earthlink.net

Making music makes you smarter!

Profession: Piano coach
Name: Bobbie Jo Sims
Company: Bobbie Jo Sims
Country: USA

Coaching children to enjoy music as they become accomplished piano players means bringing out their creative potential while instilling self-discipline and confidence. This card, using springlike splashes of color, establishes a pleasing left-right balance between the work and the fun, while the motto, "Light your creative spark," makes the connection between them.

It's a keeper because:
◆ Bright colors appeal to creativity, sans serif text to technique
◆ Creative and classic motifs are balanced
◆ Use of white space gives feeling of innocence and clarity

Profession: Stationery designer
Name: Jane A. Flavell
Company: Gordon Flavell and Company
Country: Scotland

A designer of Scottish stationery uses a multicolor tartan splash to make a cultural point and show off design skills and printing standards with this attractive card.

GORDON FLAVELL AND COMPANY
Designers and Manufacturers
of Scottish Stationery

JANE A. FLAVELL

HATTONBURN HOUSE,MILNATHORT,
KINROSS SHIRE, KY13 7SA, SCOTLAND.

TEL: 01577 862814 FAX: 01577 865676 INT. CODE +44 1577
EMAIL: tartan@flavell.com

It's a keeper because:
◆ Color scheme is perfectly appropriate to specialty
◆ Company name stands out in contrasting color
◆ Casual typeface beneath company name lightens formal feel of the card

Profession: Aquarium supply
Name: Jonas Almén
Company: Happy Fish Sverige AB
Country: Sweden

This company hires out and maintains aquariums for offices, which makes the bright graphic very much to the point. The motto beneath gives added incentive for doing business with this company.

It's a keeper because:

- Graphic echoes the vibrancy of tropical fish colors
- Lighthearted feel of card alludes to lightening up the office scene
- Rectangular graphic balances text at top of card

Jonas Almén

Happy Fish Sverige AB
Riksdalersgatan 21
414 81 Göteborg, Sweden
Tel:+46 31 41 01 36
Fax:+46 31 41 01 43
jonas.almen@happyfish.se

www.**happyfish**.se

Don't worry – Be happy!

Profession: Business trainer & consultant
Name: Jeffrey Tobe
Company: Coloring Outside the Lines
Country: USA

This card has a "reverse splash" — a black swatch on bright-colored stock. This countercurrent theme fits the owner's professional specialty.

It's a keeper because:

- Unusual color treatment lends instant recognition
- Reversed-out logo is self-explanatory
- "Primary Colorer" title piques interest

The Picture Card

<big>7</big>

Based on the mathematical principle that a picture is worth a thousand words, many business owners illustrate their cards with photographs or drawings depicting themselves, their offices, or their products or services. Adding such representations engages more senses; for example, pictures of food may elicit smell or taste memories. They also engage the mind in ways that mere words cannot, as when a familiar work of fine art is used to connote a company's attitude toward tradition and quality.

In a more prosaic sense, showing your own face on your card helps you connect on a more personal level with a customer or prospect — in effect, it brings you out from behind the counter. A mug shot also makes it easier for contacts to recognize you the next time you meet, or to remember what products or services your business offers. A product picture card can be a palm-sized, portable showroom, a quick way to display the benefits a customer can expect to receive.

Here's what's distinctive about a picture card:

- ◆ It includes a personal photo or industry-specific graphic.
- ◆ It's often printed in full color on both sides.
- ◆ Layout and design tend to be more creative.
- ◆ Folded, oversize, and other unusual formats are more common.

A picture or photograph should be sharp and have colors as true as possible. This usually means higher costs for design, layout, materials, and printing. Having committed to a higher budget, many picture-card users break other card design boundaries as well. Picture cards are more likely to be seen in larger sizes or nonstandard formats, such as folded "minibrochures."

An illustrated card is a good way to create immediate recognition for people, products, or concepts, providing a ready connection between your name and your face or product. It's a shortcut to a higher comfort level with prospects that can, in turn, translate into a natural edge over your competitors.

Real estate agents are especially aware of the value of pictures, like the one you see below. Theirs was the first industry (other than professional photographers) to make pictures on cards an almost universal practice. It helps people put a name with a face, and as any sales professional knows, getting into the prospect's memory gives you a strong competitive edge.

Profession: Real estate
Name: Bobbie Miller
Company: E-N Realty
Country: USA

A photo portrait personalizes this real estate broker's card, an important function in a profession that requires familiarity, confidence, and trust. The colors of the graphic and the gold foil spelling out the corporate name balance each other diagonally across the card.

It's a keeper because:

◆ Portrait personalizes the service

◆ Design communicates strength, stability, reliability

◆ Agent's name stands out near her picture

Profession: **Health products**
Name: **Heather Hanthorn**
Company: **Shaklee**
Country: **USA**

A finely rendered drawing can sometimes be more effective than a photograph. This card has a soft touch that enhances the personal nature of the products. "Handwritten" script front and back further personalizes the card and gives the card integrity.

nutritional supplements   sports nutrition line

anti-aging skin care line

environmentally sound   personal care
cleaners   products

Helping People Feel Great Since 1956!

It's a keeper because:

◆ Hand-drawn artwork personalizes the message

◆ Contact info is prominent, easy to read

◆ Product lines are listed on the back

Profession: **Personal & corporate coaching**
Name: **Veronica Lim**
Company: **Veronica Lim Ltd**
Country: **UK**

A photo portrait integrated into a sleek graphic give this elegant card a sense of controlled power, movement, and change — from darkness into light. The effect is enhanced by the right-aligned text and the address framing the bottom of the card.

It's a keeper because:

◆ Portrait personalizes the service

◆ Design communicates strength, focus, direction

◆ Simplicity and white space highlight contact info

Kevin Fleming
p h o t o g r a p h y

Post Office Box 156 • Rehoboth Beach, Delaware 19971
kfleming@dmv.com • www.photographysource.com
telephone 302 227 4994 • fax 302 226 8885

It's a keeper because:

◆ Service is demonstrated directly on the card

◆ Owner's name is shown directly beneath his work

◆ Magazine covers greatly enhance credibility

Profession: Photography
Name: Kevin Fleming
Company: Kevin Fleming Photography
Country: USA

This photographer's card shows off some of his work for highly regarded magazines — demonstrating both his craft and his reputation. The colorful artwork draws immediate attention, and the contact information is in plain sight.

Profession: Hospitality
Name: Rosie & Kingsley Knott
Company: Willunga House Bed & Breakfast
Country: Australia

WILLUNGA HOUSE
BED
&
BREAKFAST

State Heritage listed accommodation in the McLaren Vale Wine Region

Rosie and Kingsley Knott
1 St Peter's Terrace, Willunga
South Australia 5172
Telephone (08) 85562467
Please use area code even when calling from (08) areas
Facsimile (08) 85562465

The graceful, friendly façade of this inn invites the reader to come inside and relax. The additional allure of staying in a historical structure, and in a popular destination, enhances the message, and the vital contact information is available at a glance.

It's a keeper because:

◆ Photo gives immediate impression of relaxed setting

◆ Historical designation adds reason to visit

◆ Type is clear and easy to read

Profession: Bookkeeping
Name: Carol J. Hartman
Company: J & D Business
Services, Inc.
Country: USA

The photograph and tag line say it all: "We make life less taxing!" so you can hang onto your money. The text in this very direct card is laid out symmetrically within the white space to balance the powerful graphic, and the position of the fingers leads the eye to the president's name.

It's a keeper because:

◆ Layout of graphic and text is well integrated
◆ Graphic carries powerful message
◆ Font variations highlight specific information

Profession: Consulting & marketing
Name: Adrian Stores
Company: Acrobat Consulting & Marketing Ltd
Country: UK

Extra help that can perform amazing feats is what this card offers, in both company name and graphic. On the reverse, the logo hints at the company's agility, while contact information below is spaced out and easy to read.

It's a keeper because:

◆ Eye-catching logo, graphic, and company name work well together
◆ Two inks inexpensively give impression of full color
◆ Vertical layout gives feeling of agility

"...like an egg carton on wheels"

Profession: Moving & storage
Name: Uri Cohen
Company: On-line Moving &
Storage
Country: USA

The photo composite of a truck with an egg-carton load bed is obviously about the care taken with personal items being moved. Both the nature of the business and the promise of service are implied. The folded-over format leaves plenty of room for the distinctive logo and vital contact information.

It's a keeper because:

◆ Design and graphics echo memory hook
◆ Unusual format makes card stand out

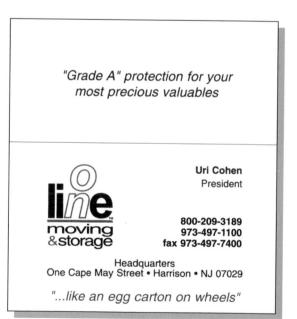

*"Grade A" protection for your
most precious valuables*

Uri Cohen
President

800-209-3189
973-497-1100
fax 973-497-7400

Headquarters
One Cape May Street • Harrison • NJ 07029

"...like an egg carton on wheels"

Profession: Attorney
Name: Eric E. Meyer
Company: Kell Alterman &
Runstein, LLP
Country: USA

This is a card-and-a-third with a photo of the lawyer inside the fold. The historical building portrayed on the outside and the overall gold color imply tradition, respectability, and success. The back of the card lists the company's practice groups.

It's a keeper because:
- Graphics and color give impression of solidity
- Layout is professional outside, personal inside
- Practice specialties are spelled out on reverse

Profession: Printing
Name: Vernon Young
Company: Pitscards
Country: UK

Using a variety of cards to promote his business-card business, this owner shows the utility of both a photo portrait and a caricature in personalizing his materials. The reverse delineates reasons for the recipient to purchase his products, including "instant recognition."

It's a keeper because:

- The caricature is amusing but provides recognition
- Card is an attention-getter
- Business-card utility is aptly demonstrated

Profession: Publishing
Name: Nicholas Reardon
Company: Reardon Publishing
Country: UK

The oversized card this publisher has created not only stands out in a crowd of other cards, it fits the idea of the great outdoors, which is his publishing field. The second color, green, accents this specialty, and the caricature adds to the casual feel.

It's a keeper because:

◆ Simple, unsophisticated style fits village setting and outdoor themes

◆ Caricature of owner hiking in mountains adds touch of humor, further humanizes business and owner

◆ Larger-than-usual size makes card stand out

Profession: Mortgage lender
Name: Bob & Naoko Sutterfield
Company: Sutterfield Mortgage
Country: USA

In a card that looks like a million bucks, this portrait of a couple of happy "loan arrangers" in the presidential oval immediately sets a friendly, jovial tone. "By appointment and referral only" indicates the exclusive nature of their business, and the company philosphy on the reverse adds even more credibility.

It's a keeper because:

◆ "Cash" look stands out in a book of cards
◆ Photo and philosophy build trust
◆ Service guarantee is printed on reverse

Your Mortgage Lenders for Life

By Referral Only Means:

We dedicate 100% of our time and energy servicing our clients to their satisfaction. This unique concept has allowed us to build strong, lasting, lifetime relationships. You can expect to receive the same Super Service all of our customers have received. We specialize in creative loan solutions, solving your mortgage needs on a personalized level, service that you could not get elsewhere. Our friendship continues after the close of your loan and we hope we have earned the right and privilege to ask you for your heartfelt endorsements to your family, friends and work associates. This is what Referral Only means. We want to be Your Lenders For Life.

When you absolutely, positively have to have loan approval, call us, we Guarantee:

A. *Loan approval*   B. *30 day close*   C. *Payment amount as quoted*

Member of: National Mortgage Brokers, Hawaii Association of Mortgage Brokers, Business Network International • Toll free (Outer islands & Mainland) 1-888-BOB-4YOU • Email Bob@bob4you.com

Profession: Entertainment
Name: Stan Heimowitz
Company: CelebrityGems
Country: USA

Everybody wants celebrities at his birthday bash or office party, and this company supplies them — or reasonable facsimiles of well-known people. The cartoon on the front of this card caricatures some of the faux celebs available. All the contact information is out of the way, on the back.

It's a keeper because:

◆ Caricatures give an idea of impersonators available
◆ Color picture is interesting in itself
◆ Putting contact information on back leaves one side for picture only

CelebrityGems

* Corporate Events
* Private Parties
* Fund-Raisers

STAN HEIMOWITZ
4061 E CASTRO VALLEY BLVD
#118
CASTRO VALLEY
CALIFORNIA 94552-4840
(510) 581-5964
CelebGems@aol.com

★ ★ ★ ★ ★ ★ ★ ★ ★ ★ ★ ★
When you think entertainment,
think Celebrity Gems.

SQUADRON LEADER
JOHN PAIGE
THE RED ARROWS

RAFC CRANWELL SLEAFORD, LINCOLN NG34 8HB
TEL: **01400 261201** EXT **7062** FAX: 01400 261120
DIRECT TEL/FAX: **01400 261120**

Profession: Squadron leader
Name: John Paige
Company: The Red Arrows
Country: UK

This formation-flying jet pilot has a card like no other, showing where he works when he's on the job. The bright red airplane would be a real attention-grabber anywhere, and it leads the eye to the contact information. Paige's picture is in a thumbnail on the back.

It's a keeper because:
◆ Red jet plane grabs attention
◆ Military look of emblems lends credibility

The Full-Color Card

The Full-Color Card

8

Immediate visual impact is the goal of the full-color card. The attention-getting device on this kind of business card is not the bright swatch or the elegant white space, but maximum coverage of the card with color and dramatic images. It often uses the same format and size as a basic card, but goes in the opposite direction in terms of graphic design, images, colors, coverage, and fonts. The look is slick and commercial.

Unlike splash cards, most full-color cards are totally covered with design elements. The inks bleed to all edges, and contact information is either printed on top of color or reversed out. Rather than containing a logo or symbolic image surrounded or balanced by white space and text, a full-color card often consists of a striking edge-to-edge image, almost like a magazine cover in miniature, on one or both sides. Although the card format is similar to basic and classic cards, the look is casual and kinetic, rather than composed and conservative. If classic is suit and tie or slacks and turtleneck, the full-color card is blue jeans and tennis shoes.

In a typical full-color card —

◆ At least one entire side of a card is printed in color

◆ Printing is by four-color process

◆ Size and stock are standard, not specialty

◆ Use of nonstandard, specialty, or display fonts, as in ads and magazine covers, is more common

A full-color card is designed to get people to pick it up and look at it. Once they've done that, they usually take note of the business represented and keep the card for future reference — or perhaps pass it along as a conversation piece.

If you decide to budget for a full-color card, be careful not to let the design overwhelm your message. Your name and profession should be readily apparent, even when printed over or reversed out of a complex image, and contact information should not be hard to locate or read.

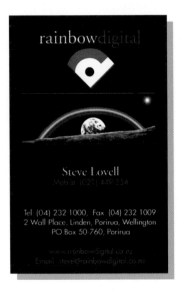

Profession: Digital printing
Name: Steve Lovell
Company: Rainbow Digital Ltd
Country: New Zealand

Rainbow Digital's card is a perfect demonstration of the quality of its services. The striking photomontage of moonscape and rainbow is printed on a glossy black background. The logo and contact information frame the scene, and the list of services on the reverse is clean and easy to read.

It's a keeper because:

◆ Dramatic design and color contrast demand attention

◆ Alignment of company name, logo, and photo lead eye to owner's name

◆ Print quality demonstrates company's capabilities

◆ Reversed type is easy to read

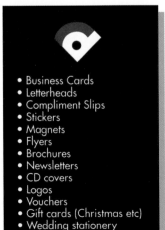

- Business Cards
- Letterheads
- Compliment Slips
- Stickers
- Magnets
- Flyers
- Brochures
- Newsletters
- CD covers
- Logos
- Vouchers
- Gift cards (Christmas etc)
- Wedding stationery
- Web sites

Profession: Magazine editor
Name: Alicia Teo
Company: Elisher Communi-
cations
Country: Singapore

This is a clean, crisp use of full color in a geometrically balanced card. The vivid colors attract the eye, and the simple icons communicate the message effectively. The quoted line alludes to the company's philosophy and the importance of its services.

It's a keeper because:

◆ Design gives sense of service approach
◆ Use of color in company name is playful, attractive
◆ Color bars at upper left stand out in card file

Profession: Designer
Name: Phil Turner
Company: 4 Design
Country: UK

The subtle use of dark maroon fields on both sides gives this glossy card a restrained power, demonstrating the company's understated design approach. The metallic-inked logo is the main element, but the name and contact information come readily to the eye.

It's a keeper because:

◆ Dramatic use of single color hints at design approach
◆ Logo placement is designed for card files
◆ Icon on back keys to phone number

Profession: Graphic design
Name: Sandy Jones
Company: S. L. Jones Design
Company
Country: USA

The front of this company's card shows some of the "infinite possibilities for your graphics" that are mentioned on the monocolor reverse (along with job specialties and contact information).

It's a keeper because:

◆ Rich colors enhance dreamlike effect of front

◆ Design is repeated on back in shades of gray

◆ Logo and list of specialties give professional look

Profession: Graphic design
Name: Chriss Coe
Company: Crisgraf Design
Country: USA

Using the owner's name as a pun for a familiar brand of shortening, this card displays Chriss Coe's sense of humor and makes an eye-catching and oddly familiar marketing tool. The card is likely to be kept handy to show friends, many of whom will be impressed by Coe's computer skills.

It's a keeper because:

◆ Name, logo, and memory hook work well together

◆ Card is likely to be passed around and talked about

◆ Design demonstrates owner's artistic skills and sensibilities

Profession: Printing
Name: Brian Ballard
Company: Harlequin
Country: Australia

A business card echoing a vintage graphic style makes an effective tool for a printer demonstrating the quality of his work. His specialties are listed on the black-and-white reverse (not shown) along with his memory hook: "Creative Ideas with Words & Pictures."

It's a keeper because:

◆ Harlequin figure implies skill, dexterity
◆ Graphic echoes memory hook
◆ Use of single ink on back cuts printing cost

Profession: Artist
Name: Laurie Mireau
Company: MireauArt
Country: Canada

Everything you need to know is on the front of this attractive, single-sided card: a sample of the artist's watercolor work, along with her name and easy-to-read contact information.

It's a keeper because:

◆ Layout, colors are attractive
◆ Picture displays the artists's skill
◆ Reversed-out contact information is easy to read on dark blue background

Profession: Air conditioning
Name: Hj. Md Salleh Anis
Company: York Air Conditioners
Country: Malaysia

The color transition from warm to cool tells what this product is all about, and in the tropics, air conditioning is a hot seller. Samples of the products are shown on the front, contact information on the back.

It's a keeper because:

◆ Design of the card is integrated with the function and value of the product

◆ Colors on front attract attention

◆ Use of color touches on back helps distinguish product logos

Profession: Design & printing
Name: Jerry Lund
Company: Lund Media
Country: USA

It's a keeper because:

◆ Bold color bars make card stand out in a crowd

◆ Back of card makes clever use of single color in text design

◆ Design aptly illustrates one service available

The colors jump out at you from a distance, and there are only a few unobtrusive lines of contact information to distract you — except the owner's name, which is turned 90 degrees and reversed out of black. The back of the card is similarly inventive with a listing of services. It's a clean design and an effective card.

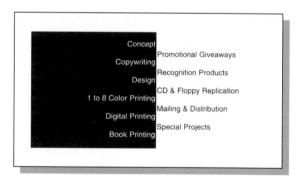

Profession: Interactive products
Name: Kristin Wiggins
Company: Gyro Design Group
Country: USA

The whirlpool of its gyroscopic logo draws you into this vivid, high-tech, satin-finished card. Contact information is presented in a clean, square-blocked font that reinforces the impression of machinelike precision. The design is echoed in reverse on the other side, where the cardholder's name appears.

It's a keeper because:

◆ Front and back designs are well integrated
◆ Colors and fonts imply efficiency
◆ Gyro graphic pulls attention into center of card

Profession: Software training
Name: Penny Edge
Company: Page Training Ltd
Country: UK

Although the country manor shown on the front is Old World, the services revealed behind the "turned-down" corner are 21st century. An attractive map on the back shows the cardholder how to get there.

It's a keeper because:

◆ Elements of design are about tradition and progress
◆ Faux corner draws eye to service listing
◆ Subdued colors provide calm, understated feel
◆ Simple, clear map shows location

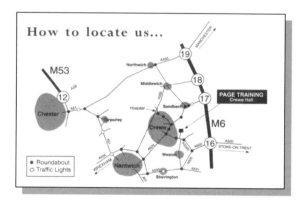

Profession: Design consulting
Name: Evelyn Hardie
Company: The Puffin Room
Country: UK

On this striking, matte-finished card, the one bright color, that of the bird's feet, is used to highlight the company name and, on the reverse, the company's services. It's an understated look that implies quality and confidence.

It's a keeper because:

◆ Single bright color cues important information
◆ Attractive design promotes design team's talents
◆ Overall look is professional

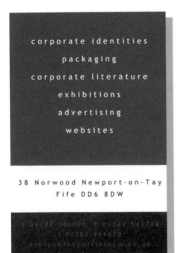

Profession: Graphic design
Name: Colleen
Company: Layout & Design
Concepts
Country: USA

Nothing catches your eye faster than a card that stares back at you. This one is likely to be noticed and passed around, to the benefit of its owner, a graphic designer. The memory hook is a neat double entendre.

It's a keeper because:

◆ Eyes are strong attractor
◆ Memory hook works two ways

Profession: Graphic design
Name: Jeff Bacon
Company: Image Sign & Design
Country: USA

The image on this card is so convincingly rendered that it looks embossed and covered with dew, but it's only a masterful illusion. The diagonal logo hooks the viewer, who then turns the card a quarter-turn to read name and contact information.

It's a keeper because:

◆ Bright, contrasting colors make the image pop
◆ Off-kilter design says "creative"
◆ Contact information in large type is easy to read
◆ It's likely to be passed around

Profession: Graphic design
Name: Ken Cawthorne
Company: Drawcard Design Group
Country: Australia

Another creative design from down under, this graphic design company's card has rich colors, high gloss, and a pleasing geometric motif. The plastic feel, front and back, makes it pleasant to handle. It's vivid enough to come to your attention again and again.

It's a keeper because:

◆ Vivid colors attract attention, show off studio's design skills and values

◆ Services are listed on reverse

◆ Single color on back works for information, cuts expense

DRAWCARD DESIGN GROUP
*offers a cost effective design
and print management service
specialising in:*

• Advertising creation
• Brochures
• Proof reading
• Copy writing
• Logo development
• Corporate image
• Promotional products
service to your door

Profession: Design & printing
Name: Feroshia Knight
Company: Agent 47
Country: USA

This is a wild card that jumps a lot of fences. The bold, embossed graphic on the front looks and feels like metal. Information is concentrated near the bottom edge but is still easy to read. The format in front is landscape; in back, it's portrait. It's an attention-grabber, and a real showcase of the owner's capabilities.

It's a keeper because:

◆ Strong color and contrast make it about as vivid as a card can be

◆ Dynamic design communicates speed and high performance

◆ Quirky name and images stir curiosity

◆ It will probably be shared

Profession: Audiovisual equipment rental
Name: Pär Nyman
Company: Adav Rental
Country: Sweden

This slim card from an audiovisual equipment rental business has a very clean, modern design with a bold, semi-abstract logo. The overall feel is of confidence and competence.

It's a keeper because:

◆ Attention is attracted immediately to the bold logo
◆ Contact information is centered, easily readable
◆ Card owner and company name are highlighted

Profession: Corporate leadership training
Name: Bea Düring
Company: Change Maker
Country: Sweden

Another bold card from Sweden, this one used by a corporate consulting business. The bright geometric figure on a black background makes the card stand out, and text printed in three different orientations piques the interest.

It's a keeper because:

◆ Bright, bold design immediately draws the eye
◆ Contact information is highlighted on light background

The Tactile Card

9

The business card is, of course, primarily a visual tool for engaging a prospect's mind. Its colors and graphics stimulate the eye and the imagination; the text provides the reasons and means for prospects to contact you. But there's another sense that a card engages when it's put into use: the sense of touch.

When you hand your card to others, they touch it, but in most cases they pay no attention to how it feels. However, if something about it feels unusual, they quickly become aware of this, and the added sensory input gives the card extra impact. A card that is smooth, satiny, flexible, or otherwise interesting to touch will be remembered.

This extra sensory dimension can be especially useful if the card is made of some material that has to do with your business — metal, leather, plastic, wood, or the like. You'll see several examples of such unique cards in this chapter.

The sense of touch also has to do with edges. A card that is cut to an unusual shape or uniquely folded is instantly intriguing for the recipient's hand. A folded card can also be more versatile in delivering visual information.

As distinguished from an ordinary card, a tactile card

- Often is printed on material other than paper
- Can sometimes be printed on a material that is directly related to the business
- May have an unusual shape or edge contour due to folding or die cutting

A tactile card typically involves higher costs, but the added investment gives you a way to appeal to more than the usual number of senses — usually, sight alone — that the business card engages. The way your card feels can make it memorable, the kind of object that people like to pass around and talk about. And if it's made of a special material that you process or sell, it can be a natural showcase for your service or business.

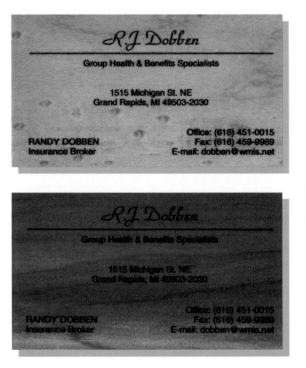

Profession: Insurance broker
Name: Randy Dobben
Company: R. J. Dobben Group
        Health & Benefits
        Specialists
Country: USA

These wood-grained cards are actually made of wood — bird's-eye maple (top) and eastern red cedar. They have a pleasing feel and are good at attracting attention. The layout is basic, but the material used gives them a classic look.

It's a keeper because:
◆ The texture is distinctive
◆ It can be carried and used like a paper card
◆ Conservative look fits profession

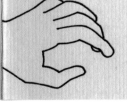

Profession: Massage
      Name: Ron McKnight
  Company: Center for Thera-
              peutic Massage &
              Acupuncture, Inc.
   Country: USA

When this folded, die-cut card is closed, the hands clasp each other. The vital information is inside. Anyone who sees this card is sure to open and close it a few times. It's a unique and creative card with a surprising amount of information.

It's a keeper because:

◆ "Hands" theme fits the profession, massage therapy
◆ Except for unique shape, it is simple and straightforward
◆ Contact info and list of services are easy to read
◆ Back of card doubles as appointment reminder

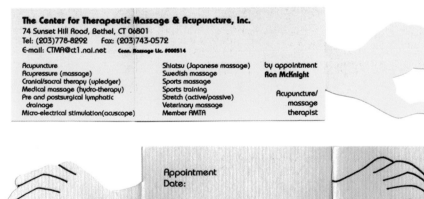

The Center for Therapeutic Massage & Acupuncture, Inc.
74 Sunset Hill Road, Bethel, CT 06801
Tel: (203)778-8292   Fax: (203)743-0572
E-mail: CTMA@ct1.nai.net   Conn. Massage Lic. #000514

Acupuncture	Shiatsu (Japanese massage)	by appointment
Acupressure (massage)	Swedish massage	**Ron McKnight**
Cranial/sacral therapy (upledger)	Sports massage	
Medical massage (hydro-therapy)	Sports training	
Pre and postsurgical lymphatic	Stretch (active/passive)	Acupuncture/
drainage	Veterinary massage	massage
Micro-electrical stimulation(acuscope)	Member AMTA	therapist

Appointment
Date:

Time:

Profession: Graphic design
Name: Paul Prisco
Company: Dog Food Design
Country: USA

It's a keeper because:

◆ Bright colors and layout are distinctive

◆ Corrugated texture makes it interesting to handle

◆ Creative design appeals to target market

"Dog Food" is an unusual name for a design firm, and the corrugated texture makes the card even more distinctive. The rough-and-ready feel brings to mind a bold marketing style, reinforcing the quirky memory hook that's found just beneath the eye-catching graphic. The vividly colored back has a distinctive treatment for the contact information, too.

Profession: Pest control
Name: Jay & Nancy Jorns
Company: J N J Pest Control &
Grounds Care
Country: USA

If termites are making your house look like this, you may want to phone the number shown. This card is a good conversation starter that's bound to be remembered when the need arises. The wood grain is printed on die-cut card stock.

It's a keeper because:
◆ Gnawed-edge look is good for a laugh
◆ Card is memorable and to the point
◆ Contour makes it easy to find in a stack of cards

Profession: Development coach
Name: Tony Gedge
Company: Bridge the Gap
Country: UK

The ultra-clean design and the semitransparent parchment stock give this card a smooth, cool feel that is pleasant to the touch as well as the eye. It seems to promise serenity through personal and professional development.

It's a keeper because:
◆ Feel of parchment stock is pleasant, substantial
◆ Classic design is simple, clean, elegant
◆ Overall look and feel enhance the implied benefits

Profession: Staffing services
Name: Danny Guidry
Company: Teramar Staffing
Systems
Country: USA

It's a keeper because:

◆ Extra edge makes it findable by feel

◆ Hole represents a need the company can fill

◆ Clean design is attractive and professional

The only thing unusual about this clean, attractive card is the hole cut through the logo, but even this small extra edge is enough to make the card retrievable by feel alone. On the back, you see that the hole represents a staffing need that can be filled by calling a toll-free number.

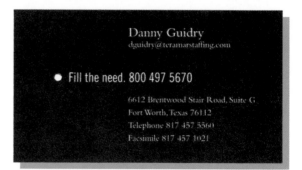

Profession: Marketing
Name: Dann Ilicic
Company: WOW! Branding
Country: Canada

It's rare to see a card made of metal, especially one that's cut into a drawing template for the company's logo. Both the texture and the shape of the brushed steel plate make it unique and memorable. It's a powerful demonstration of this company's ability to help your business achieve name recognition.

It's a keeper because:

◆ Steel cards are more likely to be passed around and commented on than ordinary cards
◆ Stencil template connotes company's branding services
◆ "Perceptionist" title is distinctive, intriguing

Profession: Flooring
Name: Eric Alexander
Company: Scandia Fine Wood Floors
Country: USA

What better way to promote your business than by using your own materials? Anyone holding this wooden card is instantly reminded of the look and feel of a fine wood floor.

It's a keeper because:

◆ Company's materials are on display
◆ Card serves as memory hook
◆ Print quality is high despite nontraditional card stock

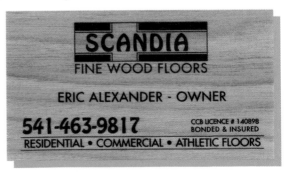

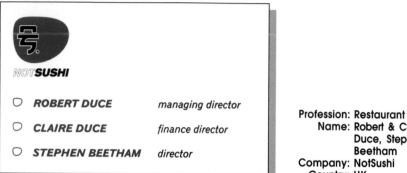

Profession: Restaurant
Name: Robert & Clair
Duce, Stephen
Beetham
Company: NotSushi
Country: UK

Despite what its name implies, this "Japanese Fusion" restaurant serves sushi and a lot more. The durable plastic stock has a luxurious, substantial feel that goes with the contemporary graphic design and won't get dog-eared or dirty.

It's a keeper because:

- ◆ Dark orange print on cream stock is attractive
- ◆ It promotes three members of the company
- ◆ Plastic stock stays clean, befitting food industry
- ◆ Japanese character promotes cuisine specialty

○ **CONTACT ME**   *unit 1, imperial court,*
exchange street east,
liverpool, L2 3PH

○ **PHONE ME**   *+44 (0)151 236 0643*
○ **FAX ME**   *+44 (0)1704 834933*

○ **SEND ME EMAIL**   *zen@notsushi.com*

○ **VISIT MY SITE**   *www.notsushi.com*

Profession: Pet therapy
Name: Jag Orth
Company: Jag Orth P.T.D.
Country: USA

Jag Orth, the canine pictured on the front of this uniquely engaging card, is a pet therapy dog whose mission is to improve the lives of humans. This card is already "dog-eared," the prominent features of the subject having been cut so that they stand out above the fold. Inside, Jag invites us to "howl at my human, Lisa Orth," to schedule appointments.

Jag Orth P.T.D.
Siberian Husky - Pet Therapy Dog

phone   503-429-3018
cell   503-709-1513
dog-mail jag@autotrolltd.com

Pet Therapy
Jag provides opportunities for therapeutic, motivational, educational and/or recreational benefits to enhance quality of life.

Crisis Response
Jag is trained to recognize and respond to people that are in emotional and/or traumatic shock. This type of trauma is usually associated with events such as natural disasters, shootings and automobile accidents.

It's a keeper because:
◆ Cut and fold make the card uniquely fitting
◆ Being invited by the dog is great "soft sell"
◆ Blue highlight in dog's eye uses two-color process to best advantage

I am a Delta Certified Pet Therapy and Crisis Response Team Dog. I help teach kids about pet safety and I'm a good listener!!

Howl at my human, Lisa Orth, to schedule our services

phone   503-429-3018
cell   503-709-1513
dog-mail jag@autotrolltd.com

References available upon request.

(tc) design by tcgrafx@imagina.com

Profession: Design & printing
Name: Eileen Tham
Company: From Design to Print
Country: Singapore

The glossy surface of this durable plastic card sends a message of technical skill and professional reliability. Both front and back take full advantage of the rainbow for an attractive presentation of the company's services and products.

It's a keeper because:

◆ Sturdy plastic stock will stay clean, uncreased
◆ Colorful design demonstrates mastery of printing technology
◆ Use of different colors makes contact info stand out

Jennifer Leacock
Sales Executive

Building #7 · Newton Industrial Park · Christ Church · Barbados · W.I.
T - (246) 420 5776 · F - (246) 420 5779 · E - sales@haltongraphics.com

Profession: Graphic design
Name: Jennifer Leacock
Company: Halton Graphics Ltd
Country: Barbados

The most distinctive feature of this delicately tinted card is its nobbly surface texture, which feels a little like fine leather. The graded eggshell color enhances the impression of luxury.

It's a keeper because:

- Texture is pleasing to the touch
- Colorful graphic stands out in otherwise reserved design
- Company name in casual script gives relaxed feel

Profession: Photographic services
Name: Orest Iwaszko
Company: Orion Photography, Laminating, Framing
Country: Canada

High-quality print stock feels like a glossy photo and shows off the services of this photographic services business. The design of the card is clean and bold with hints of artistry and craftsmanship.

It's a keeper because:

- Materials used demonstrate company's services
- Texture is pleasant, familiar
- Surface is durable, stays clean
- Single bright ink is used effectively to highlight logo

Photography · Laminating · Framing
Orest Iwaszko
17 John St. W, Oshawa, Ontario, L1H 1W8
Bus.:(905)434-3824 Fax:(905)434-7064

Profession: Advertising
Name: Charles B. Tomasello
Company: American Sales Co.
Country: USA

When you pick up this card, you first notice how light, smooth, and flexible it is. But the real surprise hits when you tilt it back and forth and see

It's a keeper because:

◆ It will be passed around and talked about

◆ It's interactive

◆ The calendar makes it even more of a keeper

◆ It's a self-advertising card

the Statue of Liberty standing in 3-D before a full-color American flag, with the names of the states popping from the red stripes. Unfortunately, you have to see it in person — the hologram can't be reproduced using an ordinary printing process.

Charles B. Tomasello
AMERICAN SALES CO.
Authorized Century Club Dealer of
KAESER & BLAIR
**Promotional Advertising
Products**

3215 Chapel Rd.
Spring Arbor, MI 49283
(517) 750-4070
Phone & Fax
Toll Free
1-877-750-3461

www.americansalescompany.com

The Multipurpose Card

10

If you think back on the cards you've seen so far in this book and elsewhere, you'll realize that the ones you remember best are those that are distinctly different from the others in the way they look or feel, or that carry a unique message. But there's another way to make a card memorable: make it serve more than one purpose.

A multipurpose card

- ◆ Gives the same essential contact information as other cards
- ◆ Provides other benefits as well — usually a special service, a discount, a handy note card, or an appointment reminder
- ◆ Is usually printed with graphics or pictures, in color, on both sides
- ◆ Is often folded or oversized to provide space for additional uses

Many service providers use cards that double as appointment reminders. When you have one of these, you tend to keep it around for days or weeks until your appointment is history. By then, you're thoroughly familiar with the card's look, feel, and message, so you're likely to remember that provider the next time you need that kind of service.

Oversized, folded cards can serve as handy note pads. If you're having lunch with a prospect and hand him this kind of card, he may start jotting notes on it so he can remember what you're saying. In effect, he signs on as a free marketing specialist, personalizing the card's message for himself in a way that you could not have anticipated when you printed it.

Another way to make your card a keeper is to design it as a buying incentive. "Present this card for a free gift (or discount)" means the card will travel, not just gather dust in a drawer or card file. Of course, this also means it's less likely to be given away. If you give one to Joe or Jane, hand over another two or three to be given to friends.

A multipurpose card doesn't have to be fancy or expensive, but it will necessarily cost a bit more if it uses a nonstandard card size or is folded. A standard-size card that simply offers discounts or premiums can cost exactly the same as one that does not.

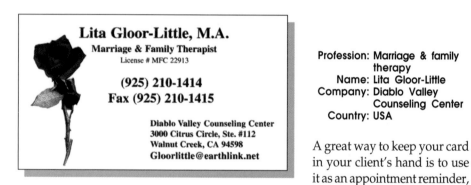

Profession: Marriage & family therapy
Name: Lita Gloor-Little
Company: Diablo Valley Counseling Center
Country: USA

A great way to keep your card in your client's hand is to use it as an appointment reminder, as on the back of this card. The simple, attractive graphic and the therapist's license number on the front number provide emotional reassurance.

It's a keeper because:

♦ Simple, understated design has appropriate emotional tone

♦ Appointment reminder keeps card at hand

♦ License number adds credibility

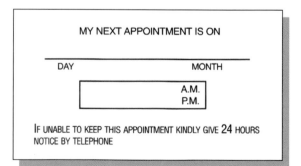

Profession: Cleaning services
Name: Rosa
Company: Rosa's Cleaning Service
Country: USA

For a card that folds into a standard size, this example has a lot of uses. Inside the fold you can specify what items you want cleaned, and Rosa can write in her charges. On the back are spaces for appointment dates, regular charges, and first-time charges, along with a list of services. This card is a whole file drawer unto itself.

It's a keeper because:

◆ Listing years of experience adds to credibility
◆ Service requests are documented
◆ Card serves as appointment reminder
◆ Simple folded card serves many purposes

Special Requests	Charge	Other Requests	Charge
☐ Windows			
☐ Verticals			
☐ Mini blinds			
☐ Steam clean carpets			
☐ Upholstery			
☐ Inside Refrigerator			
☐ Inside oven			

First appointment ——————
Next appointment ——————
First Time Charge ——————
Regular Charge ——————
Cleaning Personnel:

_____

_____

We tailor our service to fit your needs.

dusting • vacuuming • mopping
kitchens • bathrooms • baseboards
window sills • spot clean walls
vacuum furniture

If unable to keep appointments, please give 72 hours notice. Appointments not cancelled in advance are subject to 1/2 of your regular cleaning charge.

805-522-6171 or 805-522-8591 (Fax)

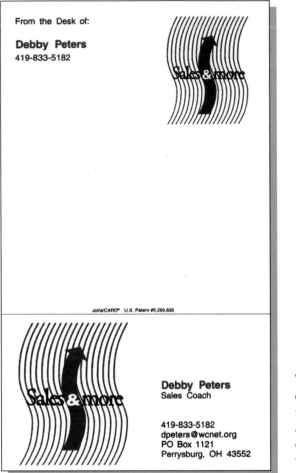

From the Desk of:

Debby Peters
419-833-5182

Jot/a/CARD® U.S. Patent #5,299,835

Debby Peters
Sales Coach

419-833-5182
dpeters@wcnet.org
PO Box 1121
Perrysburg, OH 43552

Profession: Sales coaching
Name: Debby Peters
Company: Sales & More
Country: USA

This business card with a note card attached is a handy tool to have around when making a sales pitch. When separated, one part goes into the Rolodex, while the larger part, with the notes, gets carried around. Both parts have the owner's name and phone number for easy referral. The design is clean and attractive, with plenty of white space for notes.

It's a keeper because:

◆ When separated, it becomes a standard card and a note card
◆ Simple design, no fold, single-sided printing keep costs down
◆ It provide plenty of room to take notes without writing on card

Profession: Seminars
      & marketing
Name: Geoffrey Kirkwood
Company: The "Time Out"
      Seminar Company
Country: Australia

THE 'TIME OUT'!
SEMINAR COMPANY

Geoffrey Kirkwood
Marketing Director

Telephone: 07 3348 4600
Facsimile: 07 3348 4611
Email: geoff@tosc.com.au
P.O. Box 761 Hamilton Central Qld 4007

The back of this eye-catching card has spaces for notes, seminar dates and times, or any other information the holder wishes to record. The whistle says "coaching," and the clock embedded in the "O" nicely plays off the company name.

It's a keeper because:

◆ Bright colors, clean layout attract the eye

◆ Visual pun accents company name

◆ Graphic ties in general idea of coaching

◆ Back of card is useful for taking notes

Taking **'Time Out'** to Work Smarter In Your Business

SEMINARS   SPEAKERS   MARKETING

VALERIE JEFFERYS M IDM FFMSc

BAYSTRAIT HOUSE STATION ROAD BIGGLESWADE BEDS SG18 8AL
TEL: 01767 601470 FAX: 01767 312323 e-mail: val@ultimedia-m.co.uk
DIRECT TEL: 01767 601621

Profession: Marketing
Name: Valerie Jefferys
Company: Ultimedia Market-
ing Limited
Country: UK

Bold design, vivid colors, and a triple fold make this card a true mini-brochure. Its six panels contain contact information and credentials, a list of services, the company's philosophy, testimonials from clients, space for documenting discussion topics, and a customer guarantee that is hard to pass up. In addition, the card stock is significantly heavier than standard, lending extra "weight" to the presentation.

The whole thing folds into the size of a standard business card, making it easy to handle and convenient to carry around in a cardholder.

The secret of successful media coverage is not just writing a good press release but knowing how to get it published.

Customer Guarantee

Your first press release will be *FREE* if we fail to get it published.

Contact us on 01767 601470 for full details.

ULTIMEDIA
MARKETING LIMITED

We met on

....

at ....

and discussed

call me on ....

"Overnight we had the resources of an experienced and professional team carrying out public relations, marketing and promotional activities which fully support the aims of our sales department"
David McGee
Fibre Optech Ltd

"Since we appointed Ultimedia, our average weekly sales enquiries have increased by over 20%"
Tony Hacker
Endoline Machinery

"I would gladly sell my house and children for the benefit of Ultimedia - they are that good!"
Paul Beasley ACII
RHG Corporate Insurance Group

It's a keeper because:

◆ It serves multiple purposes: business card, marketing brochure, and note card

◆ Bold design, bright colors cause it to be noticed

◆ Client testimonials are an unusual feature on a business card

◆ Standard-sized card with all essential contact information can be detached

CARE ENOUGH

TO SHARE

Profession: Dentistry
Name: Arthur V. McAuley
Company: Arthur V. McAuley, D.D.S., F.A.G.D.
Country: USA

This card is a great example of a referral source tool. It's a gift certificate that's good for a nearly free dental exam and consultation. Not only does it bring the dentist new patients, it's a thoughtful way for any-one to help someone she cares about. Attractive and friendly, it works as both a business card and a gift.

It's a keeper because:

◆ It's a gift that is sure to bring in new business
◆ The balanced, conservative design is just right for calming nervous patients
◆ The unusual size and shape make it stand out
◆ Cover phrase raises curiosity about what's inside

Gift Certificate

Good for Exam, Consultation
and Bite-wing X-Rays (if needed)
for
New Patients.

There will be a $1.00 charge to you
with this card.

PRESENT THIS CERTIFICATE
AT YOUR APPOINTMENT
❧
GIFT GIVEN BY

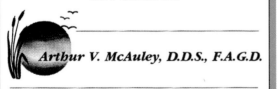

Arthur V. McAuley, D.D.S., F.A.G.D.

MEDICAL ARTS CENTER • 581 PLEASANT ST. • PAXTON, MA 01612
(508)755-2905

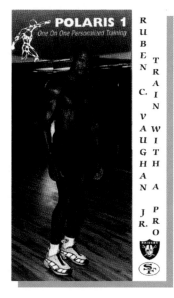

Profession: Physical training
     Name: Ruben C. Vaughan Jr.
Company: Sports Connection
 Country: USA

Along with useful information about the owner's experience, business philosophy, and service specialties, this card offers a free training session and the invitation to "train with a pro" — all on a folded card with a full-length photo of the owner, a former Oakland Raider defensive end. Its no-nonsense approach leaves no doubt that this guy is all business.

RUBEN C. VAUGHAN JR.
Oakland Raider Defensive End

• Graduated Colorado University
• Majored in Physical Ed/
  Physical Therapy
• 4 Years College Football,
  All American for 2 Years
• San Francisco 49er
• Oakland/LA Raider

As a professional athlete I learned how to condition both mind and body. I now utilize that knowledge and experience to train, motivate and educate others.

It's a keeper because:

◆ It offers a free trial session
◆ The overall look is down-to-earth, not fancy
◆ It contains a lot of useful informaion for making a buying decision
◆ The full-color panel works well with black-and-white text

ONE ON ONE PERSONAL TRAINING

Pre/post natal - A controlled workout to Maintain a body weight and fitness level that are safe for you and your baby.

Rehabilitation - Safe recovery from injury as well as improving overall fitness level.

Sports Conditioning - Amateur or professional, marathon, triathlon, or body building.

Body Sculpting - Have the physique you've always dreamed of.

Nutrition Counseling - Lose or gain weight! I can provided the specialized diet that will work with your goals and busy lifestyle.

Personal Training - The personalized attention of a one on one trainer to guide you through your workouts and maximize your potential.

I can assist in healing an injury, gaining or losing weight, or getting in shape and maintaining a good physical exercise program. I personally guarantee your satisfaction, because I'm confident that my program will work for you!

IF YOU'RE INTERESTED IN A
BETTER YOU...
A PLAN THAT WILL AFFECT POSITIVELY
EVERY ASPECT OF YOUR LIFE;
MENTALLY, PHYSICALLY, AND SOCIALLY,
THEN GIVE ME A CALL AND RECEIVE A

NO OBLIGATION

**FREE
TRAINING SESSION**

925-340-0258
SPORTS CONNECTION
100 Coggins Drive
Walnut Creek, CA 94552
925-938-5370

BEFORE   AFTER
Pete Laval lost 50 lbs. in 4 months and gained
a whole new outlook on life. So can you!

Profession: CPR training
Name: Hank Childers
Company: Ace
Country: USA

Here's a card that is sure to save at least a few lives. It's a ready reference to CPR procedures for adults, children, and infants. Many will keep it close at hand, and the instructor's name will burn itself into their memory.

It's a keeper because:

◆ It keeps the instructor's name in sight
◆ It serves a vital function in addition to promotion
◆ It's simple and straightforward

CPR Ready Reference

	Adults	Children	Infants
Rescue breathing, victim has a pulse - Give 1 breath every	5-6 seconds	3 seconds	3 seconds
No pulse- Locate compression landmark	Trace ribs into notch, one finger on sternum	Trace ribs into notch, one finger on sternum	One finger width below nipple line
Compressions are performed with	2 hands stacked heel of one hand on sternum	Heel of one hand on sternum	2 or 3 fingers on sternum
Rate of compressions per minute	80-100	100	At least 100
Compression depth	1½ - 2"	1 - 1½"	½ - 1"
Ratio compressions to breaths - 1 rescuer 2 rescuers	15:2 5:1	5:1 5:1	5:1 5:1

Profession: Real estate
Name: Celinda Chapman
Company: The Equity Group, Inc.
Country: USA

This real-estate agent is sure to generate referrals from the businesses on the back of the card who gain customers through the discounts offered. It's especially useful because it's a tough, plastic card that will stay clean and uncreased far beyond its expiration date — and the agent's portrait won't fade away in the washing machine.

It's a keeper because:

◆ "Valued Customer Card" label gives impression the company is donating the special services

◆ All essential contact information is on front

◆ Attractive, friendly photo personalizes agent and service

at the Royal College of Surgeons in Ireland

and

restaurant

MAURICE SUPPLE
General Manager

Mercer Street Lower, Dublin 2.
Tel: 353 1 478 2179
Fax: 353 1 478 0328
E-Mail: mercsi@iol.ie
www.mercerhotel.ie

Profession: Hospitality
Name: Maurice Supple
Company: Mercer Hotel
Country: Ireland

This hotel manager's card will be appreciated by guests who take walking tours through the nearby streets. It has a well-drawn, easy-to-read map on the back.

It's a keeper because:

♦ It's a clean, elegant card that leaves a good impression of the business
♦ The map on the back is well designed and useful

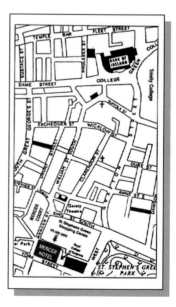

The Series Card

11

Some businesses and individuals find it useful to print and distribute not just one card but a series. Businesses that have more than one target market are an example; they need a card for each audience. Suppose you're a marketing consultant: when you approach an auto dealership organization, you don't want to hand them the same card you would give to a cosmetics distributor or a grocery store chain.

Another use for a series of cards is to promote several different products or services that you provide. If you're an office equipment retailer, you may have a card promoting computer hardware for one audience and another card for those looking for office furniture.

A series can be used as an explicit marketing tool by providing a benefit to anyone who brings in a complete set. For example, make it clear that any customer who brings you all ten of your cards by a stated deadline gets a special prize or gift. You'll have people talking to other people, and trading cards, to complete their sets.

Series cards take advantage of a quirk of human nature: people like to collect things. Even when there's no immediate return for doing so, people collect items they think may have greater value in the future, or that simply pique their interest or curiosity. Stamps, coins, license plates, and baseball cards all have their following.

People are especially drawn to any item that is turned out in a number of different versions. That's why series business cards are especially likely to be kept around; if people happen to have two or three, they start keeping an eye out for numbers four, five, and six, and then they want the whole series. It's a sure thing that your cards will be kept and admired for a long time — especially if they're real attention-getters in the first place. In fact, you'll probably get calls from people who have seen your cards and want to start their own collection.

A series card can be

- ◆ A collection of cards that one business uses to appeal to different target markets or to promote different products or services

- ◆ A group of cards that are essentially for the same market but that use different designs to encourage people to complete their collection

- ◆ A card set that provides a particular benefit, such as a gift or deep discount, to anyone who brings in a complete collection

The cost of a series of cards is variable, but most collectible cards are of higher quality in terms of printing, color, pictures, or graphics. The more cards in your series, the higher the cost, but incremental costs for each variation are normally less than for a single card. Usually, parts of the design are common to all the cards in a series; this not only maintains the integrity of your marketing image, it holds down printing costs.

Profession: Graphic design
Name: Brian J. Clayden,
Janice McLean
Company: Artisan Art & Prints
Inc.
Country: Canada

This company's artistic values are strikingly symbolized by the classic works of art, such as Michelangelo's *David*, that adorn its series of cards. It is easy to see why anyone would like to have the entire series, and why that person would contact the owner when in the market for graphic design.

They're keepers because:

◆ It's visually appealing
◆ People like to collect cards that are this attractive
◆ It's an excellent demonstration of the owner's design skills

**Patricia
Buck
Hamilton**

Fine Art Pastel Paintings

909 Carlisle Street
CO Springs, CO 80907
719-473-6333
www.PBHArt.com

Profession: Artist
Name: Patricia Buck
Hamilton
Company: PBH Art
Country: USA

The artist who created these pastels is gaining a lot of good exposure for her work by printing them on a series of business cards. Although the format varies, these cards show the same simplicity of design and adroit use of white space to frame the richly colored artwork.

"Almost Home"

PBH Art

909 Carlisle Street
CO Springs, CO 80907
719-473-6333
www.PBHArt.com

Patricia Buck Hamilton
Artist/Owner

They're keepers because:

◆ The beauty of the artist's work stands out in a simple design
◆ People who collect the entire series are more likely to see a painting that appeals to them
◆ The cards are likely to be shown to others

Profession: Specialty printing
Name: Marty Weitzman,
Company: Beyond Tomorrow
Classics
Country: USA

Here are three examples of lenticular cards that, when tilted slowly forward and backward, show either animation or different images. Although it's impossible to see in conventionally printed images, when tilted at various angles these cards display, respectively, the waterfront of St. Louis, Missouri, the owner's name and contact information, and a brief list of services; a running cheetah, a flying creature, and the owner's phone number; and a rapidly approaching steamship. This kind of card is a true conversation piece that is likely to be passed around time and time again.

They're keepers because:

- ◆ Illusion of motion catches the eye and imagination
- ◆ Plenty of information can be stored in the various images
- ◆ Images can be tied to particular professions
- ◆ They're fun to play with

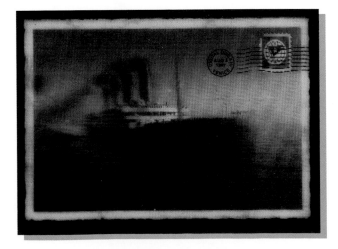

Profession: Graphic design
Name: Cliff Fisher
Company: nsomnia design
Country: USA

To communicate the idea that creativity in his company is a never-ending process, this account executive has created several whimsical cards expressing the theme in different ways with words and images. The counterintuitive use of stark black and white drawings on embossed black matte stock sets up a powerful tension between design and message.

They're keepers because:

◆ It's distinctly different from any other card you've seen
◆ The same idea is expressed in a variety of ways using the same design theme
◆ It's collectible
◆ Card demonstrates the owner's design sense

Profession: Promotions
Name: Dan Hudock
Company: Blue Rhino Promo-
tions
Country: USA

Once you've collected the entire set of this businessman's
cards, you can play any card
game you like. But long before
that, if you bring him a straight
flush or a full house he will
present you a gift. It's a pretty
canny way to promote a promotions business.

They're keepers because:

◆ People will keep looking for
other cards in the set
◆ Offering a gift for a poker hand
is a good way to bring in
customers
◆ Printing the backs of standard
playing cards makes an inexpensive business card
◆ It's amusing and eye-catching

GILBERT
DESIGN & PRINT

Rusty Brooke
SALES MANAGER

Telephone: (09) 481 0070
Fax: (09) 480 0563
Mobile: 025 355 335
rusty@gee.co.nz
88 Hinemoa Street
Box 34 067, Birkenhead
Auckland, New Zealand

Profession: Design & printing
Name: Rusty Brooke
Company: Gilbert Design & Print
Country: New Zealand

A mesmerizing display of colors on a glossy plastic card distinguishes the marketing tool of this designer and printer. Each card maintains the company's image but has designs and colors keyed together on front and back. It's a stunning demonstration of the company's professional capabilities and craftsmanship, and attractive enough to keep people looking at them as through a kaleidoscope.

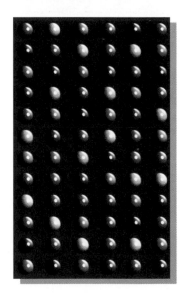

GILBERT
DESIGN & PRINT

Rusty Brooke
PRINT ADVISOR EXTRAORDINAIRE

Telephone: (09) 481 0070
Fax: (09) 480 0563
Mobile: 025 355 335
rusty@gee.co.nz
88 Hinemoa Street
Box 34 067, Birkenhead
Auckland, New Zealand

They're keepers because:

- It's a stunning display of color and printing technique
- Designs are different enough to make you look for others in the series
- Plastic stock is durable and easy to keep clean
- Use of logo maintains unity of marketing image

The Outside-the-Box Card

What law says a business card has to be a card? When you analyze the essential features of a business card, it boils down to three things:

- ◆ A business card provides vital information about the nature of your business and how to contact you, and not much else.

- ◆ A business card is intended to reach out and grab the attention of prospects, not to smother them with promotional copy like a brochure.

- ◆ A business card is compact enough to be carried around by the dozens in a card holder, suit pocket, or purse.

In other words, as long as it meets these three criteria, your most powerful miniature marketing and contact tool can be considered a "business card."

Some business owners with a lot of creative imagination have concluded that the second criterion is the most important one, and that if your objective is to create the maximum stir and get attention, liberties can be taken with usual assumptions about what constitutes a business card. And when you begin to examine and discard assumptions, you begin to think outside the box.

As you have seen in previous chapters, imaginative thinking leads quickly to an amazing variety of graphic styles, colors, card materials, card sizes, printing techniques, and other features. Continued imaginative thinking has led some to say, "Hey, if a card can be made of folded paper, why can't it be a box with something valuable or edible in it? If it can be wood or metal or plastic, why can't it be a magnet or a mirror or a CD or a mouse pad?" The answer is, it can. As long as it is in some way related to your service or product, and as long as the attention it brings you is positive, the sky's the limit.

Size and convenience are still important, of course. A box should be closer to the size of a matchbox than a boxcar, and whatever is inside should not be offensive or hazardous to adults or children. But this still leaves plenty of wiggle room, as this chapter will show you.

Expenses for an outside-the-box card depend on a lot more than design and printing costs; they are determined by other manufacturing costs, including both the packaging and the content of the item. The amount you choose to spend is limited only by the value in increased business and exposure you expect to get in return. And you should count on producing a lot of them, because if they're successful, everyone will want one.

What, then, is an outside-the-box business card? The answer can be summed up as follows:

◆   It is not an ordinary card.

So, if you want to use a business card that will open people's eyes and minds and knock the socks off your nearest competitor's marketing materials, leave your brain door open and let it run free.

Profession: Package design
Name: Linda Coppolino &
Gayle Willner-Kenter
Company: Coppolino & Kenter,
Creative Partners
Country: USA

For outside-the-box thinking, what could be simpler than a box? These packaging specialists hand out empty boxes in lieu of business cards. At trade shows, they enhance its promotional value by filling it with crayons, watercolors, or some other treat. It's an ingenious way for these partners in design to demonstrate their packaging savvy.

It's a keeper because:

◆ It's a card-sized box that promotes a packaging related business

◆ It can be filled with extras for additional interest

◆ It's an attractive design

Profession: Chocolatier
Name: Laurie Taylor
Company: Taylor Made Chocolate
Country: USA

Inside this clear plastic jewel case, behind the card, is a delicious bar of the business owner's principal product, chocolate, wrapped in gold foil. It's an irresistible sales pitch, and after you finish the treat, you've got a handy container and an attractive business card (printed with gold foil) to refer to the next time the craving strikes.

It's a keeper because:

◆ It demonstrates the owner's product directly and effectively

◆ It contains a standard business card for future reference

◆ It cannot be resisted by chocoholics

**Promotional Products &
Corporate Confectionery**

Andy Wallis

*Telephone: +44 (0)1842 761546
Fax: +44 (0)1842 754001
Mobile: 07771 593681*

*Stephenson Way, Thetford
Norfolk IP24 3RU*

Profession: Promotional products
Name: Andy Wallis
Company: Creative Sugarworks
Country: UK

Here's another box, this one from a maker of "promotional products and corporate confectionery" — in this case, card-sized boxes of candy. The front looks like a regular business card; the back tells how the product works and how to obtain some for your own business purposes.

It's a keeper because:

◆ Box and candy demonstrate their own value as a promotional tool
◆ Design is eye-catching and enticing
◆ Box is small enough to carry in a shirt pocket

HobLin Advertising Specialties

Hobart & Linda Dalton
Phone: (661) 609-1197
Fax: (661) 951-7092

Personalizit:
Photo T-shirts • Quilt Tops, Caps, Calendars, Counted Cross Stitch Patterns
Advertising Specialties:
Business Cards • Flyers • Newsletters • Letterheads
Envelopes • Tote Bags • Pens • Magnets • and Much More...

Profession: Advertising
Name: Hobart & Linda Dalton
Company: HobLin Advertising Specialties
Country: USA

It's nice to have a pocket-sized note pad handy in a pinch, and this one is fronted with a card promoting the advertising specialists who cleverly decided to use it as a promotional tool. It's a good way to ensure that their message stays before your eyes more than a few seconds.

It's a keeper because:

◆ Utility as a note pad keeps it before prospect's eyes

◆ Its use as the company's ad shows prospect its potential value

◆ Size is right for pocket or purse

Profession: Graphic design
Name: Jane Cerne
Company: Jane Cerne Graphic Design
Country: USA

This is another note pad, whose cover is an elegant specimen of classic card design, demonstrating the skill and design sense of the business owner.

It's a keeper because:

◆ Owner's design skills are ably displayed by cover card

◆ Size is handy for carrying in pocket or purse

◆ Usefulness of item keeps owner's name before prospect

JANE CERNE
GRAPHIC DESIGN

PHONE 810/695-2196
FAX 810/695-3193
wcdesign@ameritech.net

11520 SCHRAM STREET
GRAND BLANC, MICHIGAN
48439-1316

Profession: Media design
Name: John Stickels
Company: Crown NewMedia
Country: UK

It's the right size and shape, and there's contact information printed on the front, but it's got a hole in the middle and you can play it in your CD drive. When you do, you get a multimedia presentation with a lot more information about the company and its web design, print, and multimedia services. Although it looks superficially like a business card, this is a whole new tool that is taking off, especially in the high-tech industry.

It's a keeper because:

◆ It's as handy as a business card but works like an interactive brochure
◆ Even as a card, the design, layout, and information presentation work
◆ It's highly adaptable for different presentations with video, stills, animation, graphics, voice, and music
◆ Most computers now have CD drives

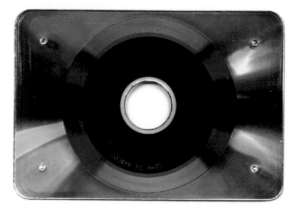

Profession: Photography
Name: Harvey Branman
Company: Photography As An Art
Country: USA

Photography As An Art
By Harvey Branman
1307 N. San Fernando Blvd.
Burbank, CA 91504
(818) 954-9294
www.harveybranman.com

If you picked up what looks like a compact with the name and contact information of a photographer on the front lid, what would you expect to see when you opened it up? In this case, you'd see your own face — there's a mirror inside. It's the photographer's way of telling you he'd be happy to take your picture.

It's a keeper because:
- It's an amusing way to promote his business
- It's useful — likely to be kept handy
- The size is right for use as a business card

Profession: Dentistry
Name: Jack Von Bulow
Company: Temple City Dental Care
Country: USA

You're checking out your smile in the mirror card above, and you see a strand of spinach caught in your teeth. What do you do? You grab this card and pull a length of dental floss out of it. As you do, you are reminded that it's about time to get your choppers checked, and perhaps the dentist who gave you this card is just the person to see.

It's a keeper because:
- It's useful in a way that connects with the business
- Almost as flat as a standard business card, it's convenient
- Sturdy white plastic is durable and easy to keep clean
- It's a great gift

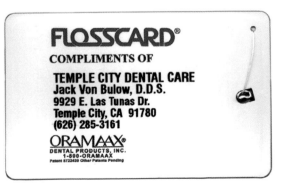

FLOSSCARD®

COMPLIMENTS OF

TEMPLE CITY DENTAL CARE
Jack Von Bulow, D.D.S.
9929 E. Las Tunas Dr.
Temple City, CA 91780
(626) 285-3161

ORAMAAX®
DENTAL PRODUCTS, INC.
1-800-ORAMAAX
Patent 5722630 Other Patents Pending

Profession: Advertising
Name: Arnie Kirkham
Company: Ad Specialties of
Oregon NW
Country: USA

When you collect all the pieces of this thin, flexible, magnetic puzzle card, it thanks you "for letting us be a part of your business puzzle." Only the phone number is given, but this unique jigsaw card, which will stick to your refrigerator, is usually accompanied by the business owner's regular card.

It's a keeper because:
◆ It's an effective visual pun on the company's message
◆ It's a refrigerator magnet
◆ People will try to collect all the pieces necessary to complete the puzzle

Arnie Kirkham

AD SPECIALTIES
OF OREGON NW

P. O. Box 1221
Molalla, OR 97038
(503) 829-2402
FAX: (503) 829-2422
adspec2@molalla.net

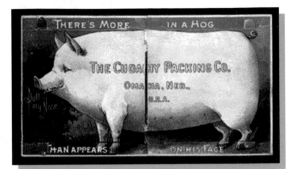

Profession: Meat packing
Name: Unknown
Company: Cudahy Packing Co.
Country: USA

Just in case you think that interactive cards are a computer-age invention, here's a trade card from Victorian times that slides open to reveal some of the many fine pork products this packing company sells.

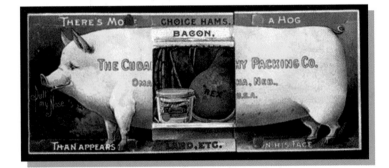

It's a keeper because:

◆ It's a valuable collector's item
◆ It shows graphically what you can get out of a hog
◆ Vivid colors immediately grab your attention

Profession: Party entertainment
Name: Ribbons the Clown
Company: Ribbons the Clown
Country: USA

Ribbons the Clown hands out a card that's almost as much fun as the clown herself. Her service specialties are listed on the ribbons, and the phone number is easy to read because your eyes are drawn to her face. This is not a card you're going to file away in your Rolodex, but who cares?

It's a keeper because:

- Ribbons attached to card are a visual memory hook for the name
- Bright colors, playful presentation are just right for a professional clown
- Service specialties use extra space on the ribbons
- It's magnetic, sticks to your refrigerator

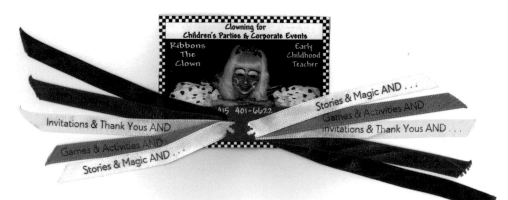

Put Your Card to Work

13

In the last twelve chapters, which have presented choice examples of what a good business card looks like, you've seen that there's an art to getting exactly the right blend of information and presentation. Perhaps you have an idea already for your next card, and you're looking forward to getting it printed and presenting it to friends, colleagues, customers, and prospects. And this is where another art comes into play — the art of exchanging business cards.

The difference between art and science is intuition. We can give you the science of business card exchange, and that's exactly what we will do in this chapter, at least a quick overview of it. The art is something you learn mostly by instinct and experience. To whom should you present your card? In what settings? During which events? Under what conditions? The finer points are a matter of feel; you know when it's right and when it's not. You become a "card artist" by listening to that inner voice and learning what feels right.

It helps, however, to learn a few guidelines first. The science of putting your business card to work can be summed up in four rules:

1. Always have plenty of business cards in your possession.
2. Know the right place to present your card.
3. Wait until the proper time to present your card.
4. Observe the etiquette of giving and receiving cards.

Keeping in mind the importance of listening to your inner voice, let's sketch an outline of the science and logic — and, to some degree, the art and etiquette — of using your business card as a contact tool.

Supply

The only place you should be caught without your business card is in the shower or bathtub. For all other occasions, here's how to make sure you have enough cards with you at all times.

◆ At home, put a large stash of cards where you keep your keys, wallet, or purse, so you'll remember to load up before you lock the door. The entry-hall mirror table is a good place; when you straighten your tie or dress on your way out the door, you'll remember to grab a handful of cards from the stack. They'll also be handy when a visitor comes to the door or a houseguest is leaving. A thousand cards is not too many to keep here; you'll use some of them every day.

◆ Place smaller stashes of 100 or more cards in other strategic locations: your office desk, your home office, the car you drive to most meetings, the glove compartment of the company van, your branch offices in other towns, your locker at the tennis club.

◆ Besides in your coat pockets or handbag, it's good practice when traveling to carry stacks of cards in your suitcase, carry-on bags, laptop case, and gym bag. Sometimes you have one piece of luggage with you but not another — in the golf clubhouse, for instance.

◆ Keep members of your network well stocked with cards — including business partners, family members, friends, vendors, and clients. The most valuable advertising you can get is a personal recommendation by someone who will vouch for you and who can instantly supply the necessary contact information.

◆ Long before you're in danger of running out of cards, order more from the printer. Just when you think you have a four-month supply left, you suddenly find yourself attending a series of conferences, seminars, trade shows, and conventions, and depleting your supply of cards before you expected to.

◆ A card that misdirects queries is worse than useless, and a card with information scratched out and hand-corrected makes you look disorganized and amateurish. Business cards are not that expensive; when your vital information changes, such as your phone number or e-mail address, round up all the obsolete cards you can and replace them immediately with new cards. This is a good opportunity to renew contact with people you haven't seen or heard from in a while. Send them a new card in a letter, explaining that while your offices have moved from the third floor to the fifth and you've established a new website, you're still available as always for help, advice, referrals, and services.

PLACE

Having made sure you're well supplied with business cards and ready to exchange them with prospective networkers and customers at every opportunity, your next move is to choose an appropriate place or event. What kind of situation should you seek? There are many, some more obvious than others.

◆ **One on one.** Whenever you meet someone new or someone you haven't seen in a while, give her your business card. This will make it easy for her to keep in touch with you, remember your profession, and think of you whenever she encounters someone who could use your products or services. Always have a card ready to hand over, and keep dozens or hundreds nearby for those times you find yourself in a crowd.

◆ **Mixers and social events.** Since your goal is to extend your network by making as many contacts as possible, be sure you have your pockets, briefcase, or handbag full of cards when you go in. These are good places to solidify and extend the local branches of your network.

◆ **Conventions and trade shows.** These events tend to bring in potential network contacts from distant cities and states. Even in trade shows for your profession, you will meet a lot of people who aren't your direct competitors. Take plenty of cards and look for opportunities to increase the reach of your network.

◆ **Other businesses.** When you visit a noncompeting business that might plausibly attract a lot of your potential customers, ask if you may leave a supply of cards to be handed out or made available. If you sell or repair sewing machines, a fabric store would be a logical card outlet. If you're a music teacher, try to get a piano tuner to hand out cards for you, and in return, distribute his cards to your clients.

◆ **International meetings and events.** If you're doing business in another country, carry two versions of your business card — one in your language and one in the language of your host country. An alternative is to print your card double-sided in both languages. If you do so, make sure that (1) the side with the second language does not look like the "backside" of your card or an afterthought, and (2) the text has been composed or carefully checked by a native speaker of that language to make sure it is error-free and says what you think it says. (If you think this latter point is not important, try assembling a toy using instructions written by someone whose acquaintance with English comes from a traveler's guide.)

◆   There are many other places and events where you can make valuable contacts, but there are also places where you should avoid any hint of business. Never send or present your business card to a house in mourning, at a wedding, or in other personal or solemn situations. Use your common sense. In what situations would you not like to have someone hand you a business card?

◆   Avoid doling out cards indiscriminately at functions that are not business related. At parties or in social situations, exchange cards in private, if at all. When you learn about the etiquette of doing business in other cultures, pay special attention to their use of business cards.

TIME

As we were told when we were growing up, there's a time and place for everything — especially a time. Be careful not to offend by presenting your card too early, or to miss an opportunity by waiting too late.

Face-to-face meetings

◆   In a business meeting, exchange cards at the beginning of the meeting. If you're meeting for the first time, this gives both of you a face-saving way to avoid the hazards of "flash-forgetting," a common phenomenon in which the other person's name evaporates from your short-term memory within three seconds of the handshake.

◆   In situations where business or social rank is a major consideration, especially in hierarchical cultures where such deference is expected and automatic, the higher-ranking person usually initiates the exchange of cards. It is a major breach of etiquette for a lower-ranking individual to offer his or her card first — somewhat like offering your hand to the queen of England.

◆   Never exchange cards during a meal. Not only are business cards not considered a legitimate course, someone you want to impress is likely to end up reading your card later through a pungent smudge of garlic and olive oil.

◆   Don't scatter your cards in a crowd and hope for the best; wait until you're face to face with each individual. Make a personal connection — a handshake, a smile, a few words — then hand the other person your card. The important thing in building and nurturing your network is to establish personal contact and make a favorable first impression. Otherwise, your card is of no more interest than one found on the sidewalk.

◆   Provide your card when asked for one, when someone offers to contact you with information, or when you are asked to repeat your name.

Contacts at a distance

◆   Whenever you communicate with someone in writing or by courier, send a card if it's appropriate to the occasion. Enclose several cards in every packet of sales material you mail out. When you send the door prize to the member who reported the most new contacts at your last meeting, enclose a card with it. Along with your thank-you note to the businessperson whose referral brought you a major contract, include a business card to replace the one she gave away, plus several more.

◆   Telephone calls are great for instant contact, but important facts tend to evaporate quickly once the connection is broken. After any telephone call in which business was discussed, follow up with a letter outlining the main points of your discussion and the action you propose to take in response — and include one or more of your cards.

◆   Do not include your card in correspondence that is personal or emotional in nature, such as a condolence card or congratulations on the birth a new grandchild. If you wish to initiate or renew business contact with this party, wait a decent interval, then find some way to offer a personal or professional favor with no expectation of anything in return. Enclose your card with this message.

ETIQUETTE

Beyond the proscriptions of place, time, and common sense when exchanging business cards, there are certain other considerations you should be familiar with. Most of these have to do with social custom rather than practical reasons.

◆   Always have cards ready at hand. Don't fish around in your pockets, your briefcase, your purse when someone asks you for a card. Keep your cards in a carrying case. As you'll see in chapter 15 ("Tools"), there are many types and styles of carrying cases that are especially designed to give you instant access to your business cards, one by one or several at a time.

◆   Your cards reflect your personality, attitude, manners, work habits, product or service quality, and business identity. They should be crisp, clean, and new. Make sure they're not wrinkled, torn, splattered with coffee, or smeared with spaghetti sauce. What would people think if you showed up wearing a suit in that condition?

◆   When presenting your card, hold it so the words can be read easily by the receiver. Keep communication uppermost in mind. You're not bestowing some fabulous gift on him, you're asking for his attention to and consideration of your message. Note, however, that in some cultures, a formal presentation is preferred, such as holding the card with both hands when presenting it.

◆   Accept your contact's card graciously. Take the time to review it and comment on some aspect of it. Show that you are paying attention and taking a personal interest, not just collecting cards. Cultural considerations are also in play here; in Japan, Singapore, Malaysia, China, and most other Asian cultures, it is customary to receive the card with both hands, examine it carefully, and formally thank the giver. It has been our experience that this formal card-giving ritual is very important. Every country has cultural idiosyncrasies, and foreign visitors who observe the rituals are appreciated for their willingness to know and understand their host culture.

◆   Don't write on a person's card in her presence. Wait until after the face-to-face contact has ended to make notes about your conversation. If you need to record important information immediately during your discussion, such as telephone numbers or other data not on the card, use your own card, and take the opportunity to hand her another or yours. (Note: if the other person presents you with a specialty card that includes space for notes or appointment times, go ahead and write on it — it's expected.)

TRICKS OF THE TRADE

People who appreciate the value of an extended network know that there are many ways to get your card into the hands and networks of others, including people you've never actually met. For these master networkers, the world is full of undiscovered opportunities. Here are a few that have been discovered lately:

◆   Learn about the personal interests of someone you'd like to
contact but have never met. When you see an item or event that

might interest him, send him a brief note and enclose your business card.

◆ When you donate used clothing, furniture, appliances, or computers to a nonprofit organization or business, drop off a few business cards as well.

◆ At a restaurant, leave a generous tip, and make sure your card is attached.

◆ Pay the highway toll for the Mercedes behind you, and leave your card for the driver.

Organize
Your
Contacts

14

Y ou've been diligent in attending network functions, making connections, getting your name before the public, and you have a mountain of business cards to prove it. Now, just about everywhere you go, you find reasons to refer people to one another.

But you've accumulated so many names, so many professions and specialties and companies, that you can't remember who does what. How can you get this jumble of valuable contacts organized in your mind? How can you keep the information at your fingertips? It can be done, but it will take some planning.

There are many ways to do it, but the system that's best for you depends mainly on two factors: the nature of your business, and the way your mind processes information. With so many different kinds of businesses, and many more kinds of minds, the way you organize networking contacts will probably be uniquely your own.

Whatever system you set up, the most important factors in maintaining it are to (1) be consistent in the way you organize and use it and (2) keep the information in it up-to-date. Each time you return from a meeting, conference, trade show, or out-of-town trip and prepare to catch up on what's happening at the office, the first item on your agenda should be to record and organize the new contact information you've gathered. Your starting point is all those new cards you've brought back with you in your pocket, briefcase, suitcase, gym bag, purse, or computer case. And if you're a really savvy networker, you will have collected several cards from each contact — three or four for use in your card filing system, and several more to use when making referrals.

Let's break the work down into three clear tasks. To integrate the new information into your existing network, you need to do three things:

1. Prioritize your contacts
2. Organize your contacts
3. Follow up on your contacts

You will follow your own inclinations, preferences, and criteria for accomplishing each of these tasks, but the end result of your efforts should always be to strengthen, extend, and enhance the effectiveness of your network of contacts. Since this is a book about business cards, we will concentrate on a system for organizing the cards you accumulate in all the networking, contact-establishing, card-exchanging activities that you do.

PRIORITIZE

Regardless of your system, the first thing you need to do is sort your contacts according to their potential importance to your network. Your time is valuable, and if you're like most people in these busy times, you have to ration it. We recommend a triage system:

The A list consists of contacts with whom you definitely want to develop relationships and maintain regular contact, whose cards you want to keep near at hand. This category can be further subdivided into three groups:

1. Prospective clients
2. People you will refer to others
3. People who will pass referrals to you

The B list is contacts whose cards you might want to keep for possible reference, but that will not be developed under any of the A-list criteria. These are people with whom you don't expect to stay in regular contact other than sending them an occasional sales letter, promotional piece, or newsletter. To simplify your filing system, it's usually best to keep these cards separate from your A-list cards.

The C list is everybody else — people or industries you don't want or expect to contact. There's no reason to keep these cards, so if you're short of desk space, throw them away. But think carefully before you toss them:

haven't we all dropped something into the trash only to regret it a day or two later? A separate card box might become a lifesaver. You can note the date of contact on the back of the card and leave it in the C box for a few months or a year, then go through periodically and cull the ones you've had longest and never used. In the meantime, your C-box cards will come in handy as bookmarks or toothpicks.

ORGANIZE

Any two-way relationship, whether personal or business, is based on a familiarity with each other's interests, skills, preferences, ambitions, desires, charitable activities, hobbies, and other factors. It is also based on making contact often enough to avoid being forgotten or ignored. These two principles guide the way your A list helps you build and maintain relationships.

Once you've done your triage and have sorted everything into three piles, you can start to organize your A-list database by alphabetizing your cards, grouping them by region or industry or profession, cross-referencing them, or applying any other criteria that fit your profession and your business habits.

There are two principal ways of setting up your database: the old way and the new way. The new way is the computer way, but we'll start with the old way, because it illustrates the principles in simple terms.

The card file database

Suppose you meet Ms. Maryellen Tellitall, who is the marketing manager of Read All About It, a growing public relations firm in a nearby city. You exchange cards. She tells you that her company specializes in profiling successful businesspeople in the sports industry. You also learn that she likes adventure travel and that her hobby is photographing exotic flowers.

When you return to your office, the first thing you do is enter these facts into your database — your card file. You've subdivided this file into three categories of information: name, type of business, and interests. Each of these categories is further subdivided.

This is where you learn why it's good to have many copies of Maryellen's card. Let's say you have at least seven. File them as follows:

◆ Your Name subfile is alphabetical. You file one card under T for "Tellitall" and another under R for "Read All About It."

♦ Your Business Type subfile is divided into twenty-odd categories, among which the most appropriate for Maryellen's card are Public Relations and Sports.

♦ Your Interest subfile has at least thirty categories, and you file the last three cards under Photography, Flowers, and Travel.

A few weeks later, you read a newspaper article about a local travel agency that has planned a group tour around a major golf tournament in New Zealand. You also learn that the area where the tournament is to be held is famous for having some of the world's most beautiful flowers. Thinking that this event might interest some of your network members, you clip the article.

Riffling through your database file, you see Maryellen's card twice, under "Sports" and "Flowers." You send her the clipping, along with your card and a note: "Thought of you when I saw this article. Perhaps there's a project here for you."

This is a prime, relationship-building contact: a business lead, a personal lead, and a reminder of you, all rolled into one. Whether the lead works out or not, you've strengthened this network relationship. She is likely to remember you the next time she encounters someone who might need your service.

If you prefer not to use multiple cards or have difficulty obtaining them, you can accomplish the same thing with a tickler file. Instead of Maryellen's cards, you write Maryellen's name and business information on a blank card and file it just as you would the real thing. When you search the categories, you'll see her name pop up the same way. Of course, this means more work for you in maintaining and updating your file.

There are several other kinds of noncomputer hardware that can be useful in different contexts. Each can be useful in a particular context but has intrinsic limitations.

Rotary desk file. If you spend most of your time working at a desk, a rotary card file is a good way to keep your contact cards at your fingertips, assuming you have them well organized. However, you can't easily carry this with you on the road, so you need another, more portable card set in order to make contacts when you're on a trip.

Business card box. A simple file with cards filed by name or industry in A–Z pockets is sometimes used as a desk accessory but, like the rotary file, is not well suited for travel.

Business card book. For carrying in a briefcase, you may find a business card book most useful, whether a pocket-sized booklet or a large, loose-leaf binder. If part of your business is referring business to others, this is a good option. BNI members carry such books constantly in their role as networking hubs.

Day planner. Most date books of this genre contain pockets for business cards. Unfortunately, because of their other functions, most day planners don't hold enough cards for someone who needs ready access to most or all of her network.

The computer database

The personal computer revolutionized data management, and one of the most widely used program types is the sortable or relational database, in which data entered are categorized in several different areas to enable sorting by different combinations of criteria. Such an application is perfect for managing contact information; instead of placing multiple copies of Maryellen Tellitall's card in different slots, you simply enter the name, business name, and other contact information into a record, then mark all relevant categories that have been chosen to appear on the data record. If the contact's interests, business specialties, or other data change, it's a simple matter to open the record on screen, make the change, and close the record.

Computer databases can be interfaced with other applications in very useful ways. For instance, the names and addresses that you've entered into your database can easily be used to address and print letters or mailing labels automatically for any selected subset of contacts or your entire database. No new information has to be added. In other words, nearly all the necessary work is done up front, and maintaining and using the system from then on, for whatever purpose, is faster and more efficient than with any card file.

If you like to see the card itself, there are a number of ways you can scan the card image into a file that can be carried on digital media and viewed onscreen or perhaps pasted into a database record that has already been created. You can buy a pocket-sized card scanner to carry with you to meetings and conferences for on-the-road convenience. There are even scanners with optical character reader (OCR) software that can convert the imaged text into true text, which automates the process of creating a data record. You can get about as high tech as your pocketbook and inclinations permit.

And who would dare get caught away from the office without his personal digital assistant (PDA)? Most can be interfaced with your main computer to download your database of contact information. On the road, it's available to you at the touch of a few buttons. You can also use your PDA to check your schedule, send and receive e-mail, write memos, calculate expenses, doodle during meetings, and get work done that you used to have to stay at the office to accomplish.

FOLLOW UP

Your filing system may differ in many respects from the ones we've talked about, but the importance of using it to make and maintain contact is vital. Write out a schedule and set goals for making contacts. You could set aside 30 minutes each day to look through your file and choose someone to call. Or you could leave the time factor open and set a goal to call 5, 10, or 20 contacts, new and old, every week. Keep an eye out for people and events you can discuss, and choose the people most likely to be interested in or able to benefit from these opportunities.

On your first contact, make it a point to offer your new networking partner the benefit of your knowledge — an event that will interest him, a hot prospect for his business that you will contact on his behalf, a special deal that you can arrange with another networker for something he needs. Always operate on the principle (outlined in Dr. Misner's book *The World's Best Known Marketing Secret* and in *Masters of Networking* by Dr. Misner and Don Morgan) that givers gain; that is, the good you do for others will eventually come back to you.

Few of the people you meet for the first time at a business mixer are going to express a need for your product or service, but that doesn't mean you have nothing to offer them. Recommend the people on your A list by distributing their cards at other functions you attend. Let them know that you've passed their card to an individual, that you've recommended their business, and that the prospect is expecting a call.

Once you've made that first contact, you need to keep building on it. One important way to do this is to follow up on previous contacts. A few weeks after your note to Maryellen, you should follow up with another note or a phone call to ask whether the referral worked out. This will remind her of your interest in her business and other pursuits. It will also reinforce her resolve to look for ways to return the favor.

Here are other occasions for calling a contact:

◆ Follow up on a topic of conversation.

◆ Request information about the contact's company.

◆ Give a referral.

- ◆ Arrange a meeting with someone the contact wants to know (and which you can attend).
- ◆ E-mail, fax, or send news or information that may be of interest to the contact.
- ◆ Invite the contact to an event.
- ◆ Send a thank-you card or congratulations on a success.

Other reasons to follow up on a first contact are aimed at letting her know more about you:

- ◆ Send your brochure.
- ◆ Call to tell her about new products or services.
- ◆ Send samples or discount coupons.
- ◆ Ask her to participate in a focus group for the launch of a new product or service.
- ◆ Invite her to be your guest at an industry-related dinner or event.

There are as many reasons to make and follow up on contacts as there are people and events combined. The important thing in developing your network is to start with the business card. Give yours away freely in the certainty that something will come of it down the line. Obtain cards from others in the knowledge that you will find some way to be of benefit to each person that you can make a part of your network.

Card
Tools &
Resources

Card
Tools &
Resources

15

In previous chapters, we've hinted at or alluded to certain tools that can help you design, produce, and use your business card to best advantage, organize your collection of other people's cards, and set up your card database for maximum networking effectiveness. This chapter will show you some of these tools and resources and talk about how you can find, acquire, and apply them.

CARD EXCHANGE TOOLS

Compact cardholder or card case. Here are two examples of a business card tool that keeps your cards clean, crisp, and ready to exchange. There are many styles available, from polished silver or brass to jeweled or cameo or leather. These examples and others can be found at www.netique.com and in most office supply stores.

Card case promotional gift. This is a nifty, pocket-sized card case that BNI members in one region of Australia use as an ingenious marketing tool. Filled with the business cards of chapter members, it is presented to prospects or new clients to promote the giver's business as well as those of other BNI chapter members.

CARD ORGANIZATION TOOLS

Business card file. If you're a serious networker, you'll need a portable card file that will hold dozens or even hundreds of cards from people you

might want to refer to others. BNI members use the Hazel card file pictured here, which holds three cards per page (several copies per card) in transparent plastic sleeves. Office Innovations offers similar Hazel files with four pockets per page, or you can opt for a three-ring binder that will hold dozens of plastic sheets with 10 card pockets each.

Any of these will fit in a briefcase, but the Hazel three- and four-card-per-page wallets are especially compact and easy to carry. All are invaluable for promoting the members of your networking group and the professions they represent. These and many similarly useful items can be found in business supply stores or on websites such as www.officeinnovations.com.

Rotary card file. A familiar fixture on many a busy manager's desk, the rotary card file (familiarly, Rolodex) can be an effective networking tool if it's kept up to date and well organized by name, profession or other criteria. You can use either a die-cut index card mount (shown) or a transparent plastic sleeve that lets you see both sides of the card.

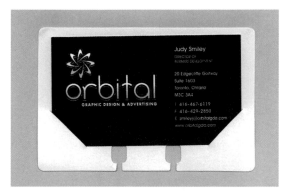

Database software. The information revolution offers many ways to automate and streamline your business card and contact information. If you're not sure which programs you might find most useful, talk with experienced colleagues, especially professional office organizers or management consultants, whose jobs require them to follow up with customers, prospects, and network members.

Here's some of the software you may find useful for your business and work style:

- ◆ ACT!
- ◆ Contact Wolf
- ◆ Goldmine Business Contact Manager
- ◆ Microsoft Access
- ◆ Microsoft Outlook
- ◆ MYCONTACT Manager
- ◆ Peachtree Contact Manager
- ◆ TeleMagic Enterprise

You can find, compare, and price many of these items on the Internet at general sales sites, such as www.pricegrabber.com, or on proprietary web pages.

Card scanner. If you collect cards by the dozens at conferences, trade shows, mixers, or sales meetings, you may find a card scanner a huge time

saver. This palm-sized device (shown: CardScan 600c, viewable at www.cardscan.com), usable anywhere there's electricity, makes an image that can be downloaded into your computer, where OCR software will read the text into your database. In researching this book, we used it to keep track of the thousands of cards we considered, along with all the businesses and professions they represented. It's a great device that we highly recommend.

CARD DISPLAY TOOLS

PR board. Any gathering of business networkers can benefit from a PR display board for attendees' cards. The BNI version pictured here has a prop in the back for placement on a table or desk. A display board is great for promoting a number of noncompeting professions and businesses simultaneously in a lobby, registration area, or waiting room, whether at an office or a trade show. If you place cards on such a board, it's a good idea

to put a stamp or sticker on the back of each to remind people of where they picked it up and why your interests and theirs coincide. This increases your likelihood of getting that first call.

Vehicle card container. If your business has a delivery or service truck that often sits unattended in public, a card dispenser attached to the outside of the vehicle is a great promotional device. This Vehicle Pocket product (www.cardpockets.com) lets people who are interested in your product or service grab a card or two as they walk by.

Business card badge. At networking gatherings, many BNI members slip their business card into this identity badge, which is manufactured by Microdyne (www.microdyneplastics.com). It lets people see your name, and if you've got a particularly interesting or intriguing card, they'll probably beg you for a few to take with them and pass along to others. Check office supply stores and websites for other types of card-insert identity badges.

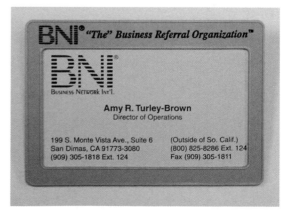

Bulletin board. In public buildings, waiting rooms, offices, and businesses, you often see bulletin boards holding items of general or special interest to employees or clients. Such a board is a good place to tack up your business card. Rather than risk offending those responsible for maintaining it, be sure to get permission to post your card or other material. A bulletin board in your own office is a handy way to draw interest, and a good place to post your brochures and extra copies of your card.

CARD ENHANCEMENT TOOLS

Stickers and stamps. For additional flexibility in using your card, print only the front, then use either pre-printed stickers or a stamp to vary the information on the back. The sticker shown here offers a chance to win a prize; it could also promote limited-time discounts, special offers, or other premiums. Printed on bright-colored stock, it's an attention-getter, too. A stamp, such as the one pictured here as used by many BNI members, is easy to apply quickly to a large number of cards. It's a handy way to help people remember where they met you, too. Just stamp a supply of cards with an event name and date, such as "Microchip Industry Trade Show, Las Vegas, November 2004." The number of possible uses is almost unlimited; stickers and stamps are an invitation to think creatively.

SUZANNE SHAFER
Independent Consultant #3162
2416 St. Rd. 236 Danville, IN 46122
317-745-1590 fax 317-271-7555
partyindy@aol.com

For a pre-recorded overview of our business opportunity,
call 1-941-655-9494 then visit our website at 1800partyshop.com

Register for $100 monthly giveaway!
www.1800partyconsultant.com/3162
or call 745-3258 × 2
Ask about our customer referral program!

Member of
BNI
BUSINESS NETWORK INT'L.

MULTI-USER CARDS

Card brochure. Here's a way to get a lot of good exposure for a group of individuals or companies: a card-sized brochure that can be separated into individual cards if desired. This is useful for noncompeting businesses in a referral group such as BNI, or for a team of associates in one organization. With a single, folded card, you can refer a whole group of your fellow networkers to a prospective client.

Invitation card. Pictured below is a card that a group of BNI chapters in Australia uses to invite a person to attend a meeting and consider becoming a chapter member. The antic group photo on the front shows the organization's spirit; on the back is the invitation, with contact information for the different groups.

CARD RESOURCES

Print shops. When you're thinking about getting new business cards printed — and you may well be, after examining all the cards in this book — you may find yourself looking for either faster or less expensive ways than going the standard print route. Large-printer orders are not overnight projects, nor are they inexpensive, but for large numbers of cards they may offer both economy of scale and quality that can't be beat. An experienced printer can help you choose materials and processes that will produce the best results with the design that you want. However, print technology is in a period of rapid change, and digital processes are coming down in cost and availability, so don't assume anything. Check out the advantages and disadvantages of alternative printing resources in your area and on the Internet.

Internet cards. Below are two excellent examples of the attractive and effective cards that you can order via the Internet at low cost — or even free, if you allow the vendor (in this case, www.Vistaprint.com) to place a small ad on the back. A search for the key words "business cards" will turn up many such sites (www.cardconnection.com is one), some of which offer extra services at additional cost. As you can see, the design quality can be high, and there is a large selection of styles that you can personalize to make a professional-looking card at relatively low cost.

PC-printed cards. If you're running out of cards and can't wait two to four weeks for that next batch from your regular printer, you have two alternatives: a quick-print shop, or your own computer and printer. If you decide the print shop price is too steep or you can't wait 24 to 48 hours, you can turn out a perfectly serviceable interim card on your own printer. Software and templates are readily available to help you with your design. You can then run perforated business card sheets (Avery and other brands) through your color or black-and-white printer, turning out perhaps 10 cards per sheet. However, the design and print quality won't be up to professional standards, so you should fill in with these do-it-yourselfers only until your new cards arrive.

Digital business cards. The computer-generated "business card" that can be attached to the bottom of your e-mail message offers a new measure of utility. When you receive a message with this kind of attachment, you can easily download the information into your contact database for later use.

Play Your Best Hand

Play Your Best Hand

16

When we decided to write this book, our goal was to show our fellow businesspeople how important it is to design, produce, and distribute an effective business card. As members of BNI, the world's largest business referral network, we wanted to get across to our members and others what a powerful and essential networking tool the business card can be.

When you bought this book, a few dollars and days ago, your expectation was probably that you would gain a few ideas on designing and printing a more attractive and interesting business card by looking at examples other businesses and individuals have found useful.

If both your expectations and ours have been realized, here's what you will have gained:

- ◆ You have learned that, inch for inch and dollar for dollar, your business card is your most powerful marketing tool if used to its full potential.

- ◆ You know more than you did before about the origins of the modern business card (maybe more than you really wanted to know, but you'll forgive us if we find it fascinating) and the functions it serves for your business.

- ◆ You've seen that the most important first step in designing your own business card is to decide exactly what your business is about and what information you need to include to make your card communicate that business identity and establish your credibility.

◆ You learned that there are many distinctive business card styles available to suit your tastes, your budget, and the nature of your business, and that the design of your card is an important factor in reinforcing your business identity and being remembered.

◆ You saw more than 10 dozen excellent examples of nine different styles of business cards and learned why they work as marketing tools for the individuals and businesses they represent.

◆ You learned valuable tips, tricks, and pointers on when, where, how, and with whom you should exchange business cards, as well as how to ensure you won't run out of them just when you need them the most.

◆ You gained insight into organizing your cards and contact information into a database that will enable you to maximize the effectiveness of your networking.

◆ You found useful information on business card tools, both hardware and software, that you can use to design, print, distribute, and display your business card, as well as organize your card and contact database.

You always knew your business card was an important tool, right? But we'll bet you didn't realize just how effective a tool it truly is, or all the things you can do to take maximum advantage of its full potential. We hope this book helps you do so. We expect that your next card will take its place as a shining example of powerful marketing tool design; that it will bring in new business by virtue of its attractiveness, uniqueness, and overall effectiveness in communicating your business identity; and that your network of business and personal contacts will expand to give you the edge over your competitors and place you at the respected forefront of your profession.

In the meantime, remember this as you look through these cards and think about your next one: business cards are not only important to your business, they can be a heck of a lot of fun.

Illustration by Mark Penta

Ivan Misner as a child

Index of Names & Professions

W

Y

About BNI

BNI (Business Network Int'l.) was founded by Dr. Ivan Misner in 1985 as a way for businesspeople to generate referrals in a structured, professional environment. The organization, now the world's largest referral network, has tens of thousands of members on almost every continent of the world. Since its inception, members of BNI have passed millions of referrals, generating billions of dollars for the participants.

The primary purpose of the organization is to pass qualified business referrals to the members. The philosophy of BNI may be summed up in two simple words: "Givers gain." If you give business to people, you will get business from them. BNI allows only one person per profession to join a chapter. The program is designed for businesspeople to develop long-term relationships, thereby creating a basis for trust and, inevitably, referrals. The mission of the organization is to teach business professionals that the word-of-mouth process is more about farming than hunting: it's about the cultivation of professional relationships in a structured business environment for the mutual benefit of all.

To visit a chapter near you, contact BNI on the Internet at bni@bni.com or visit its websites at www.bni.com.